Weaving It Together

Connecting Reading and Writing

THIRD EDITION

1

Milada Broukal

HEINLE
CENGAGE Learning

Australia • Brazil • Japan • Korea • Mexico • Singapore • Spain • United Kingdom • United States

HEINLE
CENGAGE Learning™

Weaving It Together 1: Connecting Reading and Writing, Third Edition
Milada Broukal

Publisher: Sherrise Roehr

Acquisitions Editor: Tom Jefferies

Development Editor: Catherine Black

Director of Global Marketing: Ian Martin

Director of US Marketing: Jim McDonough

Senior Product Marketing Manager: Katie Kelley

Marketing Manager: Caitlin Driscoll

Marketing Assistant: Anders Bylund

Director of Content and Media Production: Michael Burggren

Content Project Manager: Mark Rzeszutek

Print Buyer: Susan Spencer

Cover Design: Page2 LLC

Compositor: Glyph International

Photo Research: Terri Wright Design, www.terriwright.com

Library of Congress Control Number: 2009939628

ISBN-13: 978-1-4240-5603-3

ISBN-10: 1-4240-5603-9

Heinle
20 Channel Center Street
Boston, MA 02210
USA

Cengage Learning is a leading provider of customized learning solutions with office locations around the globe, including Singapore, the United Kingdom, Australia, Mexico, Brazil, and Japan. Locate your local office at: **international.cengage.com/region**

Visit Heinle online at **elt.heinle.com**

Visit our corporate website at **www.cengage.com**

Text Credits: p. 171: The poem "Rain", from Earth Magic, is used by permission of Kids Can Press Ltd., Toronto. Text © 2006 Dionne Brand.

Printed in the United States of America
2 3 4 5 6 7 11 10

Brief Contents

Contents

A Message from the Author

Approach

***Weaving It Together,* Book 1**, is the first in a four-book series that integrates reading and writing skills for students of English as a second or foreign language. The complete program includes the following books: Book 1–Beginning Level; Book 2–High Beginning Level; Book 3–Intermediate Level; and Book 4–High Intermediate Level.

The central premise of ***Weaving It Together*** is that reading and writing are interwoven and inextricable skills. Good readers write well; good writers read well. With this premise in mind, ***Weaving It Together*** has been developed to meet these objectives:

1. To combine reading and writing through a comprehensive, systematic, and engaging process designed to integrate the two effectively.
2. To provide academically bound students with serious and engaging multicultural content.
3. To promote individualized and cooperative learning within moderate- to large-sized classes.

Through its systematic approach to integrating reading and writing, ***Weaving It Together*** teaches ESL and EFL students to understand the kinds of interconnections that they need to make between reading and writing in order to achieve academic success.

Organization of the Text

***Weaving It Together,* Book 1** contains eight thematically organized units, each consisting of two interrelated chapters. Each unit begins with a set of questions to engage the student into the theme of the unit. Each chapter begins with a reading, moves on to a set of activities designed to develop critical reading skills, and culminates with a series of interactive writing exercises.

Each chapter contains the same sequence of activities:

1. **Pre-Reading and Predicting Activities:** Each chapter opens with a photograph, a set of discussion questions, and a vocabulary matching exercise. The pre-reading activity prepares students for the reading by activating their background knowledge and encouraging them to call on and share their experiences. The key vocabulary acquaints students with the words that appear in the reading.
2. **Reading:** Each reading is a high-interest passage related to the theme of the unit. Selected topics include colors, healing pets, and secret languages. The final unit includes readings from literature.

3. **Vocabulary:** Three types of vocabulary exercises practice the vocabulary contained in the reading. "Vocabulary in Context" uses the new words in the context in which they were used in the reading. "Vocabulary Building" and "Vocabulary in New Context" help students extend their vocabulary skills to new contexts by, for example, learning to recognize collocations, synonyms, or antonyms. Additionally, once per unit a "Word Partnership" box provides a complete collocation of a vocabulary word taught in that chapter. These are included to expand students' knowledge of how words go together in order to improve reading fluency.

4. **Reading Comprehension:** There are two types of exercises to check students' reading comprehension: "Looking for the Main Ideas" concentrates on a general understanding of the reading; and "Looking for Details" focuses on developing skimming and scanning skills.

5. **Discussion Questions:** Students work in small or large groups to discuss questions that arise from the reading. The discussion questions ask students to relate their experiences to what they have learned from the reading.

6. **Critical Thinking Questions:** These questions are much more challenging than the discussion questions. When students think critically about a given topic, they have to consider their own relationship to it, and thus the interaction with the topic is greater. Students interact in small or large groups to discuss or debate these questions, giving the classroom a more meaningful environment.

7. **Writing Skills:** In connection with each of the 16 readings, a different aspect of writing at the sentence level is presented. These aspects include sentence word order, capitalization and punctuation, and the use of adjectives, adverbs, and prepositions. Exercises on the points taught provide reinforcement.

8. **Student Model Essay:** Students are asked to write a paragraph, using the ideas they have generated in the discussion section and the grammar points they have practiced. The text takes them through the writing process one step at a time. First they write sentences about themselves in answer to questions presented in the text. Next students rewrite their sentences in the form of a paragraph, using a checklist (on their own or with a partner) to check their paragraphs and then making any necessary alterations. Teachers are encouraged to add to the checklist any further points they consider important. In the third step, students are encouraged to work with a partner or their teacher to correct spelling, punctuation, vocabulary, and grammar. Finally, students prepare the final version of their paragraphs.

Weaving It Together: Optional Expansion and Review Activities

The final page of each chapter, entitled "Weaving It Together," offers three types of expansion and review activities:

1. **Timed Writing:** To prepare them for exam writing, students are given a 50-minute timeframe to write sentences and practice using the paragraph format similar to the "Writing Practice" they have worked on in the unit. Teachers may change the 50-minute timeframe to one that suits their requirements.

2. **Connecting to the Internet:** These activities give students the opportunity to develop their Internet research skills. This activity may be done in a classroom setting, under the teacher's guidance, or—if students have Internet access—as a homework task leading to a classroom presentation or discussion. Students can choose from these activities: doing Internet research related to the theme of the chapter, putting ideas together for presentation in an organized way, and evaluating Websites for their reliability.

3. **What Do You Think Now?:** Students are asked to review their answers from the "What Do You Think?" questions at the start of each unit. The questions review the information they learned while completing the unit.

Journal Writing

In addition to having students do projects and exercises in the book, I strongly recommend that students be instructed to keep a journal in which they correspond with you. It gives them an opportunity to tell you what they like, what they dislike, what they understand, and what they don't understand. By having students explain what they have learned in the class, you can discover whether they understand the concepts taught and identify language concerns and trouble spots that need further review. In its finest form, journal writing becomes an active dialogue between teacher and student that permits you to learn more about your students' lives and to individualize their language instruction.

Note for the New Edition

In this new edition of **Weaving It Together, Book 1**, I have added a quiz at the beginning of each chapter to engage students in the theme of the chapter. The quiz is repeated at the end of the chapter so that students can check how much information they have learned from the chapter. In addition to the discussion questions, critical thinking discussion questions have been added to give students the opportunity to develop their thinking skills. For those who need to write under constrictions of time, a timed writing activity has been included at the end of each chapter. I have also expanded the Internet activities. I hope that you will enjoy using these new features and that **Weaving It Together** will continue to help you toward success.

Special Days

UNIT 1

What Do You Think?

Answer the questions with your best guess. Circle **Yes** or **No**.

Do you think . . .

1. in Japan, 3, 5, and 7 are lucky birthdays?	**Yes**	**No**	
2. Hindu children celebrate birthdays only until age 10?	**Yes**	**No**	
3. in China, friends and family eat noodles on birthdays?	**Yes**	**No**	
4. the Chinese New Year is always on January 21?	**Yes**	**No**	
5. Chinese children get gifts of money in orange envelopes?	**Yes**	**No**	

Chapter

1

Birthdays around the World

Pre-Reading

Discuss the answers to these questions with your classmates.

1. What do you see in the picture?
2. How is the birthday in the picture different from a birthday in your country?
3. Do you like birthdays? Why or why not?

Key Vocabulary

Do you know these words? Match the words or phrases with the meanings.

1. to celebrate _____
2. customs _____
3. to gather around _____
4. one breath _____
5. a flag _____
6. flavors _____
7. lucky _____

a. the habits of a country or group
b. to do something special and fun for a reason
c. having good things happen by chance
d. a piece of cloth with special colors for a country
e. to stand together in a group
f. special tastes
g. the amount of air that you take into your body and then let out again

Reading

Birthdays around the World

1   Everybody has a birthday. Many children in other countries **celebrate** their birthdays like children in the United States. They have a birthday cake, gifts, and sometimes a birthday party for friends. Friends and family **gather around** a table with a birthday cake on it. They sing "Happy Birthday to

5   You." Two American sisters wrote this song in 1893, but people still sing this song today! The birthday cake usually has lighted candles on it, one candle for each year of your life. The birthday child makes a wish and then blows out all the candles. If the child blows out the candles in **one breath**, the wish will come true. Other countries have different **customs**.

10   In Norway, Denmark, and Sweden, people fly the country's **flag** outside their home to tell everyone that someone in the family is having a birthday. In Denmark, a parent puts gifts around a child's bed when the child is sleeping at night. When the child wakes up in the morning, the gifts will be the first thing the child sees. In Sweden and also in Finland, the birthday child

15   gets breakfast in bed!

In some countries, some years are more important than others. In Holland, these are 5, 10, 15, 20, and 21. They call them "crown" years. On a crown birthday, the birthday child gets a much more important gift. The family also decorates the child's chair at the dining table with flowers, paper,

20   and balloons. The special years in Japan are 3, 5, and 7. These are the **lucky** years. On November 15 every year, there is a festival called "Seven, five, three" when the children and their families go to a religious place. Then the family gives a party for the child and gives the child gifts. Because of religious reasons, Hindu children only get to celebrate their birthdays until

25   the age of 16.

Birthday cakes around the world come in different sizes and **flavors**. There are even ice cream birthday cakes today. In China, there is no birthday cake. Friends and family go out to lunch, and to wish the birthday child a long life, they eat noodles!

Vocabulary

A. Vocabulary in Context

Complete the sentences. Circle the letter of the best answer.

1. Children in the United States _____ their birthday with a cake, gifts, and a birthday party.
a. celebrate b. say

2. People around the world have different birthday _____.
a. customs b. countries

3. Friends and family _____ the child and the birthday cake.
a. blow out b. gather around

4. It is sometimes not easy to blow out the candles in one _____.
a. wish b. breath

5. In Norway, Sweden, and Denmark, people put a _____ outside the house.
a. flag b. gift

6. Birthday cakes can have a chocolate _____.
a. flavor b. noodle

7. In Japan, 3, 5, and 7 are _____ years.
a. happy b. lucky

B. Vocabulary in New Context

Answer these questions with complete sentences.

1. What color is the flag of your country?

The flag of my country is red, white, and blue.

2. What other days do people celebrate?

_____

_____

3. What is your favorite flavor of ice cream?

_____

_____

4. What is a birthday custom in your country?

_____

_____

C. Vocabulary Building

Complete the sentences with the words from the box.

celebrate (_verb_)	**celebration** (_noun_)

1. We _____ my birthday with a party.

2. Every year, we have a _____ for my parents' wedding anniversary.

breathe (_verb_)	**breath** (_noun_)

3. Take a deep _____.

4. It's good to go out and _____ some fresh air.

flavor (_verb_)	**flavors** (_noun_)

5. I like the _____ of vanilla and chocolate.

6. They _____ many dishes with garlic and ginger.

Reading Comprehension

A. Looking for the Main Ideas

Read the passage again, and look for the **main ideas**. Circle the letter of the best answer.

1. Children in other countries celebrate birthdays _____.
   a. like people in the United States
   b. with just their friends
   c. in different ways

2. In Norway, Denmark, and Sweden, people _____ on a child's birthday.
   a. fly a flag
   b. have breakfast in bed
   c. put gifts in the child's bed

3. In some countries, some _____ are more important than others.
   a. cakes
   b. years
   c. festivals

4. Birthday cakes _____.
   a. are the same around the world
   b. have noodles in China
   c. are different everywhere

B. Looking for Details

Read the passage again, and look for **details**. Circle **T** if the sentence is true. Circle **F** if the sentence is false.

1. There is one candle on a birthday cake.	T	F
2. In Denmark, they put gifts around the birthday cake.	T	F
3. Two sisters wrote the famous birthday song.	T	F
4. The crown years are 5, 10, 15, 20, and 21.	T	F
5. In Finland, the child eats breakfast in bed.	T	F
6. Hindu children celebrate their birthday after age 16.	T	F

Discussion Questions

Discuss the answers to these questions with your classmates.

1. Which birthday custom in the reading do you like best? Why?
2. How do you usually celebrate a birthday in your country?
3. Are birthdays important in your country? Is another day, such as your name day or New Year's Day, more important?
4. Do you celebrate your birthday every year, or only in special years?

Critical Thinking Questions

Discuss the answers to these questions with your classmates.

1. When and why do you think birthday celebrations started?
2. Why do you think that 5, 10, 15, 20, and 21 are "crown" years in Holland? What does it mean?
3. A birthday child makes a wish. Why do you think this is done?

Writing

Writing Skills

A. The Sentence

A sentence always has a subject and a verb. Many sentences also have an object. The sentence order in English is usually as follows:

Example:

subject	verb	object
John	has	a birthday.
(subject)	(verb)	(object)

The Subject

The *subject* is usually a noun, a pronoun, or a phrase with a noun. It tells us who is doing the action and usually comes before the verb. Look at the subjects in the following sentences:

Examples:

John has a birthday. (The subject is a noun.)

He has a birthday. (The subject is a pronoun.)

The tall boy has a birthday. (The subject is a phrase with a noun.)

The tall boy with black hair has a birthday. (The prepositional phrase **with black hair** comes after the noun and is part of the whole subject.)

The Verb

The *verb* tells us the action of the subject. Some verbs are one word, but other verbs are more than one word.

Examples:

Mary <u>has</u> a birthday today. (verb)

Mary <u>is having</u> a birthday. (verb)

Mary <u>is going to have</u> a birthday tomorrow. (verb)

Punctuation and Capitalization

A sentence always begins with a capital letter and ends with either a period (.), an exclamation point (!), or a question mark (?). The first word after a comma (,) begins with a small letter.

Capitalization Rules

Here are some rules for using capital letters.

1. Capitalize the first word in a sentence.

Many children have a birthday cake on their birthday.

2. Capitalize the pronoun *I*.

John and I have the same birthday.

3. Capitalize all proper nouns. Here are some proper nouns:

a. Names of people and their titles:

Mr. John Sands	Ms. Mary Lee
Robert	Diana
Bob Briggs	Chan Lai Fong

b. Names of cities, states, and countries:

London, England	Houston, Texas
Acapulco	Hong Kong
Taiwan	Korea

c. Names of days and months:

Monday	Saturday
May	July
Friday	August

B. Exercises

1. Underline the subject in each sentence.

1. She has a brother.
2. Mary Peel loves children.
3. The tall woman has a birthday today.
4. The tall woman with white hair has a birthday today.

5. Many children have a birthday cake.

6. Birthday cakes are a custom.

7. Customs in some countries are unusual.

8. Parents in Denmark put gifts around the birthday child's bed.

2. Underline the subject with one line and the verb with two lines in the following sentences.

1. She has many gifts.

2. The child laughs.

3. The little girl is laughing.

4. The little girl with the red hair is going to laugh.

5. Many friends are going to say happy birthday.

3. Change the small letters to capital letters where necessary.

1. maria is from mexico city, mexico.

2. victor is from lima, peru.

3. ito and mayumi are from tokyo, japan.

4. the test is on monday, october 7.

5. mohammed's birthday is on tuesday, april 10.

6. wednesday, june 5, is bob's birthday.

7. my sister suzie and i were born in february.

8. mrs. lee's birthday is in december.

9. mr. brown and i are going to a party on friday.

10. i am going to milan, italy, in july.

4. Find the mistakes. There are 10 mistakes in grammar and capitalization. Find and correct them.

My birthday is on june 11. I was born in lima, peru. We has a party on my Birthday. My friends comes. My mother make a cake. I get many gift. I always happy on my birthday. It is my special Day.

Writing Practice

Write Sentences

Answer these questions with complete sentences. Use capital letters and periods where necessary.

1. What is your full name?

_____

_____

2. Where do you come from? (Give the city and country.)

_____

_____

3. When is your birthday?

_____

_____

4. What is the full name of a student in your class?

_____

_____

5. Where does he or she come from? (Give the city and country.)

_____

_____

6. When is his or her birthday?

_____

_____

7. What do you usually do on your birthday (have a birthday cake, have a party, go out)?

_____

_____

Chapter

Happy New Year!

Pre-Reading

Discuss the answers to these questions with your classmates.

1. When do you celebrate the New Year in your country?
2. What kinds of food do you eat on New Year's Eve or New Year's Day?
3. Do you go out or do you stay at home for the New Year celebration?
4. What are three things most people do on New Year's Eve or New Year's Day?

Key Vocabulary

Do you know these words? Match the words or phrases with the meanings.

1. extra _____
2. to bow _____
3. ground _____
4. forehead _____
5. empty _____
6. polite _____
7. relatives _____

a. what you walk on
b. with nobody or nothing in it
c. the part of the face above the eyes and below the hair
d. members of your family
e. showing good manners
f. more than needed
g. to lower your head to show respect

Reading

Happy New Year!

The Chinese New Year is the most important holiday for the Chinese people. For the Chinese, the New Year comes on the first day of the First Moon, between January 21 and February 19.

One week before the New Year, people start to clean their homes and buy new things. Some people paint their homes for the New Year. They buy new pictures, too. New Year's pictures often have oranges in them. In Chinese, the word for *oranges* sounds the same as the word for *gold*. It is a lucky word. People buy new clothes for the New Year. It is important to start the New Year in new clothes.

On New Year's Eve, the family gets together to eat a big meal. The meal starts late in the afternoon of New Year's Eve. There are many special dishes on the table. There are usually oranges and a dish of fish. Every family tries to eat fish. At the end of the meal, they leave some **extra** fish on the plate to bring good luck.

The New Year is an important time for the family. It is a tradition for the younger people to bow to the older people. The Chinese call this *k'ou t'ou* or kowtow. This means "to touch the **ground** with the **forehead**." Then the older people give children gifts of money in red envelopes. Red is a lucky color for the Chinese.

At midnight, there are fireworks. It is New Year's Day, or the first day of the First Moon, *Yuan Tuan*. In the morning, the shops are closed, and the streets are **empty**. People dress in their new clothes and try to be kind and **polite** to each other to start the New Year well. Later, they go to visit their friends and **relatives**.

Vocabulary

A. Vocabulary in Context

Complete the sentences. Circle the letter of the best answer.

1. At dinner, the Chinese leave some _____ fish on their plate.
a. extra   b. orange

2. Young people usually _____ to older people in China.
a. give   b. bow

3. When people bow, they lower their _____.
a. forehead   b. foot

4. In China, many people touch the _____ when they bow.
a. ground   b. picture

5. People are _____ to each other to start the New Year well.
a. happy   b. polite

6. People visit their _____ on New Year's Day.
a. sisters   b. relatives

7. In the morning of the first day of the New Year, the streets are _____.
a. important   b. empty

Word Partnership	Use **empty** with:
n.	empty **bottle**, empty **box**, empty **building**, empty **room**, empty **seat**, empty **space**, empty **stomach**

B. Vocabulary Building

Work with a partner. Read the questions and add the letters to complete the answers.

1. What is the name of this relative: your father's brother?

_____ N _____ _____ E

2. What is a polite word in English?

P L ____ A ____ ____

3. If your glass is empty, what is in it?

____ ____ T H ____ N G

4. What do you have under your forehead?

____ Y ____ B ____ ____ ____ S

C. Vocabulary in New Context

Now make a sentence with each of the **bold** words from the reading.
For example: My uncle Armando is my favorite relative.

Reading Comprehension

A. Looking for the Main Ideas

Answer these questions with complete sentences.

1. What is the most important holiday for Chinese people?

_____

_____

2. What do people do one week before the New Year?

_____

_____

3. For whom is the New Year an important time?

_____

_____

B. Looking for Details

One word in each sentence is not correct. Rewrite the sentence with the correct word.

1. The Chinese New Year comes on the first day of the First Year, between January 21 and February 19.

_____

_____

2. New Year's pictures often have family in them.

_____

_____

3. It is important to start the New Year in new homes.

_____

_____

4. Every family tries to eat meat.

_____

_____

5. The older people give children gifts of clothes in red envelopes.

_____

_____

6. At the end of the meal, people leave some oranges on the plate.

_____

_____

Discussion Questions

Discuss the answers to these questions with your classmates.

1. Are any of the New Year's customs in the reading the same as customs in your country?
2. What do people wear for the New Year in your country?
3. Do people decorate their homes or shops?
4. Do people give or get gifts on this day?
5. How is the American celebration of the New Year different from the celebration in your country (as far as you know)?

Critical Thinking Questions

Discuss the answers to these questions with your classmates.

1. Almost every culture celebrates the New Year. Why is the New Year so important? What does it mean to people?
2. Why do you think the Chinese clean their homes and buy new clothes for the New Year? Do other cultures do this too? What does it mean?
3. What does the New Year mean to you? Do you like to celebrate the New Year? Why or why not?

Writing

Writing Skills

A. Sentence Order

As you know from Chapter 1, sentence order in English is usually as follows:

> subject   verb   object

The *verb* does the action. The *subject* tells us who is doing the action. The *object* answers the question "What?"

The Object

The object can be a *noun*, a *pronoun*, or a *noun phrase*.

Example:

People	buy	new pictures.
(subject)	(verb)	(object)

Older people	give	gifts of money.
(subject)	(verb)	(object)

The Complement

Some verbs are not action verbs; they are linking verbs. Some examples are *like*, *be*, *become*, *seem*, and *feel*. These verbs may be followed by a noun, a noun phrase, or an adjective. This is called a *complement*.

Example:

The streets	are	empty.
(subject)	(verb)	(complement)

The color red	is	good luck.
(subject)	(verb)	(complement)

Punctuation and Capitalization

Remember that a sentence always begins with a capital letter and ends with a period (.), an exclamation point (!), or a question mark (?).

Capitalization Rules

Here are some more rules for using capital letters.

1. Capitalize names of nationalities, races, languages, and religions.

American	Chinese
Muslim	Catholic
Hispanic	Asian
Italian	Arab

2. Capitalize names of special days.

New Year's Day	Independence Day
Christmas	Halloween

B. Exercises

1. Underline the object or the complement in each sentence.

1. People close the shops.
2. Some people paint their homes.
3. The older people give red envelopes.
4. The Chinese New Year is important.
5. Our family prepares special food.
6. People wear their best clothes.
7. Many people visit relatives.
8. Relatives bring many gifts.

2. Change the small letters to capital letters where necessary.

1. we do not have classes during christmas and easter vacation.
2. on new year's day, we stay at home.
3. the american woman celebrated chinese new year with us.
4. in our class, we have students who are buddhist, muslim, christian, and jewish.
5. for us, new year's day is more important than christmas.
6. all over the united states on july 4, americans celebrate independence day.

3. Find the mistakes. There are 10 mistakes in grammar and capitalization. Find and correct them.

Pat and Don hutton live in boston, in the united states. They are americans. They are also christian. They celebrates christmas on december 25. It an important holiday for them.

Writing Practice

A. Write Sentences

Answer these questions with complete sentences. Use capital letters and periods where necessary.

1. What is the most important holiday in your country?

_____

_____

2. When do you celebrate it?

_____

_____

3. What do you wear on this holiday?

_____

_____

4. Where do you go?

_____

_____

5. What food do you prepare or eat?

_____

_____

6. Do you give or get gifts?

_____

_____

7. Why is this holiday important?

_____

_____

B. Rewrite in Paragraph Form

Rewrite your sentences in the form of a paragraph like the one on page 22.

Paragraph Form

It is important that you start to write using the form of a paragraph. In _Weaving It Together, Book 2_, you will learn how to write a good paragraph with a topic sentence. For now, it is important for you just to follow the format.

1. Use lined paper or a new document in a word processing program on a computer.
2. Write your name, the date, and the course number in the upper right-hand corner of the paper.
3. Write a title in the center at the top of the page. Capitalize the first word, last word, and all important words in the title. Do not capitalize _the_, _a_, _an_, or prepositions unless they begin the title.
4. Leave a one-inch margin on the left-hand side of the page. (Your teacher may ask you to leave a margin on the right-hand side also.) A word processing program will do this for you.
5. Indent the first line of every paragraph.
6. Write on every other line of the paper, or use double-spaced lines if you are using a computer.
7. Capitalize the first word in each sentence, and end each sentence with a period.

```
                                                      Name
                                                      Date
                                                      Class
                              Title

              XXXXXXXXXXXXXXXXXXXXXXXXXXXXXXXXXXXXXXXXXXXXXX

    ◯         XXXXXXXXXXXXXXXXXXXXXXXXXXXXXXXXXXXXXXXXXXXXXXXXX

              XXXXXXXXXXXXXXXXXXXXXXXXXXXXXXXXXXXXXXXXXXXXXXXX

              XXXXXXXXXXXXXXXXXXXXXXXXXXXXXXXXXXXXXXXXXXXXXXXX
```

The list below will help you check your paragraph form.

Paragraph Checklist

- ☐ Did you indent the first line?
- ☐ Did you give your paragraph a title?
- ☐ Did you write the title with a capital letter?
- ☐ Did you put the title in the center at the top of the page?
- ☐ Did you write on every other line?

C. Edit Your Paragraph

Work with a partner or your teacher to edit your sentences. Correct spelling, punctuation, vocabulary, and grammar. Use the editing checklist to help you.

Editing Checklist

- ☐ Subject in every sentence?
- ☐ Verb in every sentence?
- ☐ Words in correct order?
- ☐ Sentences begin with a capital letter?
- ☐ Sentences end with a period directly at the end of a sentence?
- ☐ Sentences have a space between them?
- ☐ Commas in the correct place?
- ☐ Wrong words?
- ☐ Spelling?
- ☐ Missing words (use insertion mark: ^)?

D. Write Your Final Copy

After you edit your paragraph, you can write the final copy.

Weaving It Together

⏱ Timed Writing

Answer these questions with complete sentences. Use capital letters and periods where necessary. You have 50 minutes to answer the questions and then rewrite them into paragraph form.

1. What is your favorite holiday or celebration? Choose a different holiday from the one you chose in "Writing Practice."
2. When is the holiday or celebration?
3. Where do you celebrate it?
4. What do you do?
5. Why is it your favorite holiday?

Connecting to the Internet

A. Look up "birthday traditions around the world" on the Internet. Tell your classmates about 3 birthday traditions that are the most interesting to you.

B. The New Year is celebrated on different days in different cultures. Go to the Internet to find out more about New Year's customs around the world. Answer these questions:
   • When is the next: Chinese New Year, Iranian New Year, Jewish New Year, and Muslim New Year?
   • When do the English celebrate the New Year?

What Do You Think Now?

Refer to page 1 at the beginning of this unit. Do you know the answers now? Complete the sentence, or circle the best answer.

1. In Japan, 3, 5, and 7 are/are not lucky birthdays.
2. Hindu children celebrate birthdays only until age _____.
3. In China, friends and family eat _____ on birthdays.
4. The Chinese New Year is/is not always on January 21.
5. Chinese children get gifts of money in _____ envelopes.

Places

What Do You Think?

Answer the questions with your best guess. Circle **Yes** or **No**.

Do you think…

1. Dubai is a country?	**Yes**	**No**
2. people can ski on snow in Dubai?	**Yes**	**No**
3. Iceland is part of Europe?	**Yes**	**No**
4. Icelanders read more books than anyone else in the world?	**Yes**	**No**
5. Icelanders don't work very hard?	**Yes**	**No**

Chapter 3

Dubai: Modern City in the Desert

Pre-Reading

Discuss the answers to these questions with your classmates.

1. What places do you know in the Middle East?
2. Do you like modern or old cities?
3. What city do you think is great? Why?

Key Vocabulary

Do you know these words? Match the words or phrases with the meanings.

1. ski _____
2. unique _____
3. have fun _____
4. artificial _____
5. theme park _____
6. in the middle of _____
7. in the shape of _____
8. looks like _____

a. not the real thing
b. in the center of
c. only one of its kind
d. with the same form or outline as
e. be nearly the same as
f. enjoy yourself
g. move on snow with long pieces of wood under your shoes
h. an amusement park with attractions that share a common special subject

Reading

Dubai

1   Dubai is a very modern city. It is **in the middle of** a hot and sandy desert. Dubai is in the United Arab Emirates on the Persian Gulf. Dubai is also the name of one of the seven emirates or states. The emirate of Dubai is not very big. It is about the size of Rhode Island, the smallest state in the United States.

5   Around 1970, Dubai became rich with oil. The population of Dubai and the city began to grow very fast. Today Dubai has a population of one million and is a growing city. New buildings are going up all over the city. Some of these new buildings are amazing. The *Burj Al Arab* hotel is **unique**. It is very tall and **looks like** a sailboat in the middle of the sea. It is also one of the world's most

10 expensive hotels. Outside the city, there are **artificial** islands. One group of islands is called *The World*. It looks like the map of the world from the sky. Homes on the islands of *The World* are only for the rich and famous. There are also the famous *Palm Islands*. These are other artificial islands. Each *Palm Island* is **in the shape of** a palm tree in the middle of the ocean. There are expensive hotels and

15 homes on the *Palm Islands*.

    You will find everything you need to **have fun** in Dubai. When the temperature is 120 degrees Fahrenheit outside, you can **ski**. There is a ski resort with snow at the Mall of the Emirates. You can also shop at the largest shopping mall in the world. For more fun, go to *Dubailand*. It's the biggest **theme park** in

20 the world. There's always an amazing building in Dubai. Maybe an underwater hotel is next.

Vocabulary

A. Vocabulary in Context

Complete the sentences. Circle the letter of the best answer.

1. Dubai is ＿＿＿＿＿＿＿ a desert.
   a. in the middle of   b. in the shape of

2. The *Burj Al Arab* hotel ＿＿＿＿＿＿＿ a sailboat.
   a. is the size of   b. looks like

3. You can ＿＿＿＿＿＿＿ at the Mall of the Emirates. You can shop or ski.
   a. have fun   b. become rich

4. Dubai has some ＿＿＿＿＿＿＿ buildings.
   a. artificial   b. unique

5. *The World* is a group of ＿＿＿＿＿＿＿ islands.
   a. fun   b. artificial

6. The islands in the *Palm Islands* are ＿＿＿＿＿＿＿ of a palm tree.
   a. in the shape of   b. in the map of

7. *Dubailand* is like Disneyland. It is a ＿＿＿＿＿＿＿.
   a. theme park   b. shopping mall

8. People like to ＿＿＿＿＿＿＿ on the snow.
   a. go up   b. ski

B. Vocabulary in New Context

Answer these questions with complete sentences.

1. What do you do to have fun?

_____

2. What building do you think is unique?

_____

3. Who do you look like?

_____

4. What is the name of a famous theme park you know of?

_____

5. Where do people to go to ski that you know about?

_____

6. What is the name of the area in the middle of your town or city?

_____

C. Vocabulary Building

Check (√) the 3 correct phrases using **have**. You may use your dictionary. Then make a sentence with each correct combination.

☐ have a problem   ☐ have difficult   ☐ have a fun

☐ have a good time   ☐ have cold   ☐ have a meal

Reading Comprehension

A. Looking for the Main Ideas

Read the passage again, and look for the **main ideas**. Circle the letter of the best answer.

1. Dubai is _____ in the United Arab Emirates.
   a. a city
   b. an emirate
   c. a city and an emirate

2. Dubai is _____.
   a. growing fast
   b. the smallest state
   c. famous for its homes

3. Dubai has many places _____.

    a. you can visit to learn history

    b. to ski in the winter

    c. for fun

B. Looking for Details

One word in each sentence is not correct. Rewrite the sentence with the correct word.

1. Dubai is in the middle of a hot and empty desert.

_____

_____

2. New hotels are going up all over the city.

_____

_____

3. The *Burj Al Arab* hotel is one of the world's most largest hotels.

_____

_____

4. One group of islands looks like the palm of the world from the sky.

_____

_____

5. Homes on the islands of *The World* are only for the rich and artificial.

_____

_____

6. When the temperature is 120 degrees Celsius, you can ski.

_____

_____

Discussion Questions

Discuss the answers to these questions with your classmates.

1. Is your city like Dubai? How is it different or similar?
2. Describe a special place (for example, a building or a park) in the city where you live now.
3. Describe a special place in another city or town you know.
4. What city or place do you want to visit one day? Why?

Critical Thinking Questions

Discuss the answers to these questions with your classmates.

1. What makes a city great?
2. Do you want to live in a city like Dubai? Why or why not?
3. Do you think people are happy in Dubai? Do beautiful buildings and shopping malls make people happy? Why or why not? Where do you think people are most happy, in the countryside or in a modern city like Dubai?

Writing

Writing Skills

A. Adjectives

Words that describe nouns are called *adjectives*. They usually answer the question "What kind?"

Examples:

Dubai is a <u>modern</u> <u>city</u>.
   (adjective) (noun)

The *Burj Al Arab* is an <u>expensive</u> <u>hotel</u>.
       (adjective) (noun)

Adjectives are the same with a singular noun or a plural noun.

Examples:

There are <u>artificial</u> <u>islands</u>.
    (adjective) (plural noun)

There are <u>modern</u> <u>buildings</u>.
    (adjective) (plural noun)

Adjectives come before nouns.

Examples:

The *Burj Al Arab* is a **tall** hotel.

New buildings are going up all over the city.

Adjectives can also come after a form of the verb *to be*.

Examples:

It is **hot** in the desert.

The *Burj Al Arab* hotel is **unique**.

B. Exercises

1. Underline the adjectives in the sentences.

1. There are expensive homes on the islands.
2. The buildings are amazing.
3. The city is in a hot desert.
4. The emirate is not big.
5. There may be an underwater hotel.

2. Put the words in the correct order.

1. Dubai / city / is / a / modern

Example: Dubai is a modern city.

2. in the middle of / Dubai / is / desert / a

_____

_____

3. all over / the city / are going up / new buildings

_____

_____

4. homes / the rich and famous / for / on the islands / are

_____

_____

3. Write about what you think. Use complete sentences. Use an adjective in each sentence.

1. What is it like in the town where you are living now?

_____

_____

2. Describe a special place in your town.

_____

_____

3. What is your school like?

_____

_____

4. What is your class like?

_____

_____

4. Find the mistakes. There are 10 mistakes in grammar and capitalization. Find and correct them.

   Dubai is a city in the middle of a desert sandy. The Emirate of Dubai is about the size of Rhode Island, the State smallest in the united states. today Dubai have a populations of one Million.

Writing Practice

A. Write Sentences

Answer these questions with complete sentences.

1. Name a city that is special to you.

_____

_____

2. Where is this city?

_____

_____

3. Describe this city using one or two adjectives.

_____

_____

4. Name one thing this city has that is special. Describe it using adjectives.

_____

_____

5. Name and describe a special building in this city.

_____

_____

B. Rewrite in Paragraph Form

Rewrite your sentences in the form of a paragraph. See page 22 for an example. Then use the paragraph checklist to check your work.

Paragraph Checklist

☐ Did you indent the first line?
☐ Did you give your paragraph a title? (Use the name of the city.)
☐ Did you write the title with a capital letter or letters?
☐ Did you put the title in the center at the top of the page?
☐ Did you write on every other line?

C. Edit Your Paragraph

Work with a partner or your teacher to edit your sentences. Check spelling, punctuation, vocabulary, and grammar. Use the editing checklist on the next page to help you.

Editing Checklist

- ☐ Subject in every sentence?
- ☐ Verb in every sentence?
- ☐ Words in correct order?
- ☐ Sentences begin with a capital letter?
- ☐ Sentences end with a period directly at the end of a sentence?
- ☐ Sentences have a space between them?
- ☐ Commas in the correct place?
- ☐ Wrong words?
- ☐ Spelling?
- ☐ Missing words (use insertion mark: ^)?

D. Write Your Final Copy

After you edit your paragraph, you can write the final copy.

Life Is Good in Iceland

Pre-Reading

Discuss the answers to these questions with your classmates.

1. Where is Iceland?

2. Is it part of Europe?

3. What do you know about life in Iceland?

Key Vocabulary

Do you know these words? Match the words or phrases with the meanings.

1. an island _____

2. a quarter of _____

3. similar to _____

4. to heat _____

5. crime _____

6. a high quality of life _____

a. 1/4 or 25% of

b. like but not exactly the same as

c. land with water all around it

d. something people may go to prison for

e. very good way of living

f. to make hot

Reading

 ## Life Is Good in Iceland

1   Iceland is **an island** in the North Atlantic Ocean. It is near Greenland and Norway, but it is part of Europe. This country has a population of about **a quarter** of a million people. Most of the people live in towns. Reykjavik is the capital and the largest city.

5   Iceland is not as cold as its name sounds. The temperature in January in Reykjavik is the same as in New York City. Icelanders speak Icelandic, which is **similar to** German, but 99% of Icelanders also speak English.

     Icelanders are the hardest workers in Europe. They work the longest hours. Many people have two or three jobs, and children work during school
10 vacations. Icelanders work hard because life is very expensive and they want a **high quality of life**. Iceland is the most expensive country in Europe. Iceland has a lot of fish, but it doesn't make cars or machines. Many of these things come from other countries. That is why they are expensive.

     Icelanders have a great system for health and education. Health care
15 and education are free. All children must go to school from age 6 to age 16. Every person in Iceland can read and write. Icelanders read a lot. Icelanders read more books than any other people in the world. Icelanders are healthy too. The air is clean in Iceland because people get natural hot water from the ground to **heat** their homes. With clean air and a good health system,
20 Icelanders live long lives. Both men and women in Iceland live the longest lives of any people in the world.

     Iceland is a great country. The air is clean. People live long. There's almost no **crime**. Icelanders have a high quality of life, but they work hard!

Vocabulary

A. Vocabulary in Context

Complete the sentences. Circle the letter of the best answer.

1. Iceland is _____, but it is also a country.
   a. an island   b. a capital

2. About _____ a million people live in Iceland.
   a. a quarter of   b. a population of

3. Iceland's language is _____ German.
   a. the same as   b. similar to

4. In Iceland, people use hot water from the ground to _____ their homes.
   a. heat   b. wash

5. There are few people in prison in Iceland because there is almost no
_____.
   a. education   b. crime

6. Icelanders like a _____ quality of life.
   a. hard   b. high

Word Partnership	Use **crime** with:
v.	**commit a** crime, **fight against** crime
adj.	**organized** crime, **terrible** crime, **violent** crime
n.	**partner in** crime, crime **prevention**, crime **scene**, crime **wave**

B. Vocabulary in New Context

Write complete sentences.

1. Name a crime.

_____

_____

2. Name something that is important for a high quality of life.

_____

_____

3. Name something that people use to heat their homes.

_____

_____

4. Name an island.

_____

_____

C. Vocabulary Building

Complete the sentences with the correct partner of the word **quality**.

air quality   quality of service   quality of life   quality of work

1. There are too many cars, and the _____ in the city is bad.
2. At the new restaurant, the _____ is very good.
3. People have a high _____ in Sweden.
4. The bag is expensive, but the _____ is very good.

Reading Comprehension

A. Looking for the Main Ideas

Answer these questions with complete sentences.

1. Where is Iceland?

_____

_____

2. Who are the hardest workers in Europe?

_____

_____

3. What kind of health and education system does Iceland have?

_____

_____

B. Looking for Details

Circle **T** if the sentence is true. Circle **F** if the sentence is false.

1. In January, Reykjavik is colder than New York City.	**T**	**F**
2. The language of Iceland is English.	**T**	**F**
3. Icelanders get their hot water from the ground.	**T**	**F**
4. Fish is expensive in Iceland.	**T**	**F**
5. Icelanders read a lot of books.	**T**	**F**
6. Children in Iceland work during school vacations.	**T**	**F**

Discussion Questions

Find students in your class who are not from your country. Then complete the chart below with information about their countries.

Country	Population	Name of Capital	Language	Special Things (foods/plants)
Iceland	1/4 of a million	Reykjavik	Icelandic	fish

Now choose a country from your chart. Use these questions to talk about that country with your classmates.

1. What can you say about the capital of the country?
2. What plants or animals does the country have a lot of?
3. What other special things does the country have?

Critical Thinking Questions

Discuss the answers to these questions with your classmates.

1. Do you think Iceland is the place for you? Why or why not? In what country do you most want to live? Why?
2. What makes a high quality of life? Is it different or the same for everyone? Explain.

Writing

Writing Skills

A. Comparing Things

We often use adjectives in comparative and superlative form to compare things and people.

The Comparative Form of Adjectives

When you compare two things that are different, use the comparative form of adjectives.

To form the comparative, add **–er** to the adjective and put **than** after the adjective.

Examples:

Iceland is **colder than** Mexico.

Mexico's population is **bigger than** the population of Iceland.

Note:	If the adjective ends in one consonant and there is one vowel before it, double the consonant:	big, bigger	hot, hotter
	If the adjective ends in **–e**, add **r**:	wide, wider	fine, finer
	If the adjective ends in **–y**, change **y** to **i** and add **–er**:	happy, happier	easy, easier

When the adjective has more than two syllables, put **more** in front of the adjective and **than** after the adjective.

Examples:

Reykjavik is **more expensive than** Paris.

Paris is **more crowded than** Reykjavik.

The Superlative Form of Adjectives

When you compare more than two things, use the superlative form of ad

To form the superlative, add **–est** to the end of the adjective.

Examples:

> Reykjavik is the **largest** city in Iceland.
>
> Icelanders are the **hardest** workers in Europe.

When the adjective has more than two syllables, add **the most** in front of the adjective.

Examples:

> Reykjavik is **the most expensive** city in Europe.
>
> Reykjavik is **the most popular** city in Iceland.

B. Exercises

1. Give the number of syllables in each adjective. Then write the comparative form.

Adjective	Syllables	Comparative Form
1. beautiful	3	more beautiful than
2. wet	_____	_____
3. dry	_____	_____
4. expensive	_____	_____
5. old	_____	_____
6. dangerous	_____	_____
7. high	_____	_____
8. large	_____	_____

2. Complete each sentence with the comparative form of the adjective in parentheses.

1. Iceland is (big) Switzerland.

_____

_____

2. Iceland is (small) Greenland.

_____

_____

3. The Pacific Ocean is (large) the Atlantic Ocean.

_____

_____

4. The Sears Tower in Chicago is (tall) the Empire State Building.

_____

_____

5. The Nile River is (long) the Mississippi.

_____

_____

6. Mexico is (dry) Canada.

_____

_____

7. The Taj Mahal is (beautiful) the Sears Tower.

_____

_____

8. Reykjavik is (expensive) Paris.

_____

_____

3. Complete each sentence with the superlative form of the adjective in parentheses.

1. Iceland has (small) population for its size in Europe.

_____

_____

2. Alaska is (big) state in the United States.

_____

_____

3. Vatican City is (small) country in the world.

_____

_____

4. Mount Everest is (high) mountain in the world.

_____

_____

5. The Nile is (long) river in the world.

_____

_____

6. Death Valley in California is (hot) place in the United States.

_____

_____

7. Tokyo is one of (expensive) cities in the world.

_____

_____

8. Acapulco is (popular) city in Mexico for tourists.

_____

_____

4. Write about what you think. Use complete sentences.

1. Which is the most interesting city to you?

_____

_____

2. Which is the most dangerous place?

_____

_____

3. Which is the most beautiful place?

_____

_____

4. Which is the largest city in your country?

_____

_____

5. Find the mistakes. There are 10 mistakes in grammar and capitalization. Find and correct them.

inga stefansson is from iceland. Iceland is a country in europe. She speak icelandic. This language is similar to german. life in Iceland is the expensivest in Europe. But people are healthy, and they live the most long lives.

Writing Practice

A. Write Sentences

Answer these questions with complete sentences.

1. Which country do you come from?

_____

_____

2. Where is your country? (Give names of countries near your country.)

_____

_____

3. What is the population of your country?

_____

_____

4. What language or languages do most people in your country speak?

_____

_____

5. What is the capital city of your country? Is it also the largest city? (If not, tell which city is the largest.)

_____

_____

6. What special things does your country have? (Name plants, foods, animals, historic places, or natural beauty.)

_____

_____

7. What can you say about your country, using a superlative adjective? (For example: _My country is the most beautiful country in the world._)

_____

_____

B. Rewrite in Paragraph Form

Rewrite your sentences in the form of a paragraph. Then use the checklist to check your work.

Paragraph Checklist

- ☐ Did you indent the first line?
- ☐ Did you give your paragraph a title?
- ☐ Did you write the title with a capital letter or letters?
- ☐ Did you put the title in the center at the top of the page?
- ☐ Did you write on every other line?

C. Edit Your Paragraph

Work with a partner or your teacher to edit your sentences. Correct spelling, punctuation, vocabulary, and grammar. Use the checklist to help you.

Editing Checklist

- ☐ Subject in every sentence?
- ☐ Verb in every sentence?
- ☐ Words in correct order?
- ☐ Sentences begin with a capital letter?
- ☐ Sentences end with a period directly at the end of a sentence?
- ☐ Sentences have a space between them?
- ☐ Commas in the correct place?
- ☐ Wrong words?
- ☐ Spelling?
- ☐ Missing words (use insertion mark: ^)?

D. Write Your Final Copy

After you edit your paragraph, you can write the final copy.

⏱ Timed Writing

Answer these questions with complete sentences. Use capital letters and periods where necessary. You have 50 minutes to answer the questions and rewrite them into paragraph form.

1. What country would you like to visit?
2. For what is this country well known or famous?
3. What language do they speak there?
4. What are the well-known cities in this country?
5. Why would you like to visit it?

Connecting to the Internet

A. Use the Internet to find interesting facts about cities around the world. Find the answers to the following questions:

- Which city has the largest population?
- Which city has the smallest population?
- What is the wettest city?
- What is the hottest city?
- What is the coldest city?
- What is the driest city?

B. Go to the Internet to find out more about Iceland. Find the answers to these questions:

- Who were the first people to live in Iceland?
- What size is Iceland?
- What is the geography of Iceland?
- What is the weather like in summer and in winter?
- What is the Golden Circle?
- What are some cultural things to do?

What Do You Think Now?

Refer to page 25 at the beginning of this unit. Do you know the answers now? Complete the sentence, or circle the best answer.

1. Dubai is a _____.
2. People can/cannot ski on snow in Dubai.
3. Iceland is part of _____.
4. Icelanders read more _____ than anyone else in the world.
5. Icelanders work/don't work very hard.

Health

What Do You Think?

Answer the questions with your best guess. Circle **Yes** or **No**.

Do you think . . .

1. sleep is more important than food?	**Yes**	**No**
2. a baby needs 12 hours of sleep a day?	**Yes**	**No**
3. your heartbeat is higher when you laugh?	**Yes**	**No**
4. every minute of laughter is the same as 45 minutes of relaxation?	**Yes**	**No**
5. there are laughter clubs where people laugh with no jokes?	**Yes**	**No**

Chapter

5

Go to Sleep!

Pre-Reading

Discuss the answers to these questions
with your classmates.

1. How much sleep do we need?
2. Do many people have problems falling asleep?
3. What do you do when you can't sleep?

Key Vocabulary

Do you know these words? Match the words or phrases with the meanings.

1. an average _____
2. to fall asleep _____
3. an adult _____
4. let's say _____
5. a statesman _____
6. an inventor _____

a. to begin to sleep
b. a person who is not a child
c. a person who is first to get an idea for something
d. what you get when you add three numbers and divide the total by three
e. suppose; imagine
f. a man who is a leader in politics

Reading

Go to Sleep!

1   **S**leep is very important. Did you know that sleep is more important than food? A person who does not sleep dies faster than a person who does not eat.

    Let's say you go to sleep 12 hours late. It will take your body about three weeks to return to normal. We spend about a third (1/3) of our lives in sleep.

5   That's about 121 days a year!

    How much sleep do we need? We are all different. A baby needs 16 hours of sleep every day. Children 6 to 12 years old need **an average** of 10 to 12 hours of sleep. Teenagers need 9 to 10 hours of sleep. **An adult** needs an average of 7 to 8 hours a night. There are some people who need only 3 hours

10   of sleep. Others need 10 hours of sleep. After the age of 50, the average sleep time goes down to 6.5 hours a night. We need less sleep as we get older.

    Most people have some nights when they cannot sleep. About one in three Americans has a problem with sleep. Many of these people cannot **fall asleep**. The name of this problem is insomnia. The word *insomnia* means

15   "no sleep." Some people say, "I didn't sleep all night." But that's not really true. They may sleep lightly and wake up several times. In the morning, they only remember the times they were awake, so they think they were awake all night.

    This is not a new problem. Many famous people in history had insomnia.

20   Some of these people had special ideas to make them sleep. Benjamin Franklin, the famous **statesman** and **inventor**, had four beds. He moved from one to the other to fall asleep. King Louis XIV of France had 413 beds and hoped to fall asleep in one of them. Mark Twain, the famous American writer, had a different way. He lay on his side across the end of the bed!

Vocabulary

A. Vocabulary in Context

Complete the sentences. Circle the letter of the best answer.

1. After the age of 50, people sleep _____ of 6.5 hours a night.
   a. an average   b. a third

2. _____ you don't sleep one day.
   a. Let's talk   b. Let's say

3. Some people cannot _____. They call this problem insomnia.
   a. get asleep   b. fall asleep

4. _____ needs an average of 7 to 8 hours of sleep every day.
   a. A teenager   b. An adult

5. Benjamin Franklin was _____.
   a. an inventor   b. a sportsman

6. Benjamin Franklin was also _____.
   a. a French king   b. a statesman

B. Vocabulary in New Context

Choose the correct answer. Then use the answer in a complete sentence.

1. Which of the following is a good thing to do to fall asleep?
   going shopping   reading a difficult book   cooking

   Example: *Reading a difficult book is a good thing to do to fall asleep.*

2. Which of the following is or was a statesman?
   Barack Obama   Pablo Picasso   Mohammed Ali

3. Which of the following was an inventor?
   Mahatma Gandhi   Thomas Edison   William Shakespeare

4. What is the average of 11, 16, and 18?
   16   15   45

5. At what age are you an adult?
   14   21   12

C. Vocabulary Building

Complete the sentences with the correct form of the new words in the box.

> **to snore** = to make noise when you sleep
> **to dream** = to see pictures in your sleep
> **to have a nightmare** = to have a bad dream

1. Sometimes I _____ in color.
2. I usually wake up when I _____. I am so scared and my heart beats fast.
3. My brother says he can't sleep because I _____ when I sleep. I don't believe him.

Now make your own sentences with *snore*, *dream*, and *have a nightmare*.

Reading Comprehension

A. Looking for the Main Ideas

Circle the letter of the best answer.

1. The number of hours we sleep _____.
   a. is the same for all adults
   b. is different for everybody
   c. gets higher as we get older

2. People who have a problem with sleep _____.
   a. are Americans
   b. are famous
   c. have insomnia

3. Benjamin Franklin, King Louis XIV of France, and Mark Twain all had _____.
   a. insomnia
   b. four beds
   c. no ideas

Circle **T** if the sentence is true. Circle **F** if the sentence is false.

1. Some people need only 3 hours of sleep a night.	T	F
2. After age 50, the average sleep time is 6.5 hours a night.	T	F
3. One in four Americans has a problem with sleep.	T	F
4. We spend about a quarter of our lives in sleep.	T	F
5. Benjamin Franklin had four beds.	T	F
6. Mark Twain was a famous statesman.	T	F

Discussion Questions

Find out from the students in your class how they sleep. Fill out the chart below.

Name	Number of Hours of Sleep Each Night	Do You Get Up in the Night?	Do You Dream?
Klara	9	sometimes	no

Discuss the answers to these questions with your classmates.

1. What do people eat or drink to help them sleep?

2. What may make you sleep badly or lose sleep?

3. What things do you need in a room to be able to sleep?

Critical Thinking Questions

Discuss the answers to these questions with your classmates.

1. What happens when people don't get enough sleep? How can one person's insomnia affect other people?

2. Imagine you need only three hours of sleep. What do you do with all that extra time?

Writing

Writing Skills

A. Using *when*

Use **when** to show that two things happen at the same time. Notice the use of the comma when the sentence starts with **when**.

Examples:

I have the lights on **when** I sleep.

When I sleep, I have the lights on.

B. Exercises

1. Join the two sentences with **when**. Begin your sentence with **when**. Use the correct punctuation.

1. I sleep. I have the radio on.

_____

_____

2. I sleep. I snore.

_____

_____

3. I sleep. I move about a lot.

_____

_____

4. I sleep. I like to hold something.

_____

_____

5. I sleep. I lie on my side.

_____

_____

6. I have problems. I cannot sleep.

_____

_____

7. I eat too much. I have a nightmare.

_____

_____

8. I am in a different bed. I cannot sleep.

_____

_____

2. Find the mistakes. There are 10 mistakes in grammar. Find and correct them.

Sleep very important is. It is most important than food. When a person do not eat, he or she dies. When a person does not sleep, he or she dies more fast. Baby need the more sleep. Teenager sleep more long than adult. People need less sleep as they get oldest.

Writing Practice

A. Write Sentences

Answer these questions with complete sentences.

1. How much sleep do you need?

_____

_____

2. What time do you usually go to bed, and what time do you get up in the morning?

_____

_____

3. Are the lights in your room on or off when you sleep? Is the window open or closed? Is your room quiet, or is there noise?

_____

_____

4. How often do you wake up in the middle of the night—every night or sometimes? What do you do when you wake up?

_____

_____

5. How do you usually sleep—on your back, side, or stomach? Do you move about a lot?

_____

_____

B. Rewrite in Paragraph Form

Rewrite your sentences in the form of a paragraph. Then use the paragraph checklist to check your work.

Paragraph Checklist

- ☐ Did you indent the first line?
- ☐ Did you give your paragraph a title?
- ☐ Did you write the title with a capital letter or letters?
- ☐ Did you put the title in the center at the top of the page?
- ☐ Did you write on every other line?

C. Edit Your Paragraph

Work with a partner or your teacher to edit your sentences. Correct spelling, punctuation, vocabulary, and grammar. Use the editing checklist to help you.

Editing Checklist

- ☐ Subject in every sentence?
- ☐ Verb in every sentence?
- ☐ Words in correct order?
- ☐ Sentences begin with a capital letter?
- ☐ Sentences end with a period directly at the end of a sentence?
- ☐ Sentences have a space between them?
- ☐ Commas in the correct place?
- ☐ Wrong words?
- ☐ Spelling?
- ☐ Missing words (use insertion mark: ^)?

D. Write Your Final Copy

After you edit your paragraph, you can write the final copy.

 Laughing Out Loud

Pre-Reading

Discuss the answers to these questions with your classmates.

1. Describe the animal in the picture.
2. Who are some well-known funny people in your country?
3. How do you feel after you laugh?

Key Vocabulary

Do you know these words? Match the words or phrases with the meanings.

1. muscles _____
2. an organ _____
3. blood pressure _____
4. heartbeat _____
5. brain _____
6. a painkiller _____
7. relaxation _____
8. circulation _____

a. measurement of the force of blood moving around the body

b. something that is not work; something that you enjoy

c. a medicine that stops pain

d. movement of the blood around the body

e. the action of the heart

f. what is on your bones that helps you move

g. a part of the body that has a special job (for example, the heart)

h. the organ in the head used for thinking

Reading

Track 6

Laughing Out Loud

1   Some people say that laughter is the best medicine. Scientists are beginning to agree with this. They are studying laughter seriously and are finding that it is really good for us.

So what happens when we laugh? We use 15 different **muscles** in our
5   face, and laughing is good for every **organ** in our body. When we laugh, we breathe quickly and exercise the face, shoulders, and chest. Our **blood pressure** goes down, and our **circulation** gets better. Our **heartbeat** is lower, and our **brain** makes a natural **painkiller** called a beta-endorphin.

Every minute we laugh is the same as 45 minutes of **relaxation**. Many
10   doctors around the world believe that laughter helps us get better when we are sick.

Today, there are laughter clubs around the world. They try to improve people's health with laughter. The laughter clubs started in India. Now they are all around the world. There are more than 450 laughter clubs just
15   in India. All kinds of people join a laughter club. They go once a day for 20 minutes and start to laugh. There are no jokes. People laugh as a kind of exercise, and everyone feels better afterwards. Some people pay a lot of money to join a laughter club and just laugh.

Of course, there are many kinds of laughter. We may change the way we
20   laugh in different situations. But we all have a laugh that is special to us. How do you usually laugh?

Here's a joke to make you laugh:

> Patient: Doctor! Doctor! Every time I drink coffee, I get a sharp pain in my eye.
> Doctor: Well, take out the spoon.

Vocabulary

A. Vocabulary in Context

Complete the sentences. Circle the letter of the best answer.

1. When we laugh, we use 15 different _____ in our face.
   a. painkillers   b. muscles

2. Laughter is good for every _____ in our body.
   a. organ   b. face

3. When we laugh, our _____ goes down.
   a. blood pressure   b. brain

4. Laughter makes our _____ better.
   a. medicine   b. circulation

5. A beta-endorphin is _____.
   a. an exercise   b. a natural painkiller

6. Laughter makes our _____ lower.
   a. chest   b. heartbeat

7. Laughter makes a natural painkiller in our _____.
   a. shoulders   b. brain

8. Forty-five minutes of _____ is the same as one minute of laughter.
   a. relaxation   b. circulation

Word Partnership	Use **blood** with:
n.	(red/white) blood **cells**, blood **clot**, blood **disease**, blood **loss**, **pool of** blood, blood **sample**, blood **stream**, blood **supply**, blood **test**, blood **transfusion**
v.	**covered in** blood, blood **stained**, **donate/give** blood

B. Vocabulary in New Context

Choose the best answer. Then use the answer in a complete sentence.

1. Which of the following is relaxation for most people?

watching television   studying   driving in traffic

2. Which of the following is an organ in the body?

a leg   a hand   the brain

3. Muscles can be found in which of the following?

our nails   our legs   our hair

4. Which of these activities makes your heartbeat faster?

sleeping   running   eating

5. What do you need a painkiller for?

a joke   a bath   a headache

C. Vocabulary Building

Complete the sentences with the correct form of the new words in the box.

---

a joke = something that you say or do that makes people laugh
to be embarrassed = to feel uncomfortable because of something you did or did not do
to burst into laughter = to suddenly begin to laugh

---

1. Some people are good at telling _____. I'm not.
2. She _____ when I told her the funny story.
3. I forgot it was her birthday. I was so _____.

Now make your own sentences with *a joke, to be embarrassed,* and to *burst into laughter*.

Reading Comprehension

A. Looking for the Main Ideas

Circle the letter of the best answer.

1. Scientists say that laughter _____.
   a. is good for us
   b. is serious
   c. is not really good

2. Laughter is good for _____.
   a. our body
   b. only the face
   c. only the chest and shoulders

3. Laughter clubs _____.
   a. are only in India
   b. are places to learn jokes
   c. help people feel better

B. Looking for Details

One word in each sentence is not correct. Rewrite the sentence with the correct word.

1. We use 50 different muscles in our face.

_____

_____

2. Laughing is good for every organ in our brain.

_____

_____

3. Every minute we laugh is the same as 45 hours of relaxation.

_____

_____

4. We may change the way we laugh in different shoulders.

_____

_____

5. When we laugh, we breathe seriously.

_____

_____

6. Our face makes a natural painkiller.

_____

_____

Discussion Questions

Find out how the students in your class laugh.

1. How many students laugh with their mouths open?
2. How many students laugh loudly?
3. How many students have a shy and quiet laugh?
4. How many students never laugh?

Critical Thinking Questions

Discuss the answers to these questions with your classmates.

1. Do you think laughter clubs are silly or important? Why?
2. Do you like to watch movies and television shows that make you laugh? Why or why not? Why are comedies so popular? What kind of comedy do you like?
3. Most laughter is good. When is laughter bad? How can laughter do harm?
4. Have you ever laughed at the wrong time? Give an example. What makes people do this?

Writing

Writing Skills

A. Adverbs

An *adverb* tells you something about a verb. It answers the question "How?" It usually comes after the verb.

Example:

When we laugh, we   <u>breathe</u> <u>quickly</u>.
                        (verb) (adverb)

We usually form an adverb by adding *-ly* to an adjective.

Example:

Adjective	Adverb
loud	loudly
quiet	quietly

B. Exercises

1. Change the adjectives in parentheses into adverbs, and rewrite the sentences.

   1. She laughs (free).

_____

_____

   2. He laughs (loud).

_____

_____

   3. She laughs (shy).

_____

_____

4. He laughs (nervous).

_____

_____

5. They are studying (serious).

_____

_____

6. He speaks (quiet).

_____

_____

2. Write five sentences about yourself, using these adverbs:

loudly   quietly   slowly
quickly   seriously

1. _____

_____

2. _____

_____

3. _____

_____

4. _____

_____

5. _____

_____

3. Find the mistakes. There are 10 mistakes in grammar and capitalization. Find and correct them.

Scientist is studying laughter serious. They are finding that laughter is goodly for us. When people are sick, laughter helps them to get more better. Laughter club started in india. People join a laughter club and go very day. They may laugh loud for minutes and feel best afterwards.

Writing Practice

A. Write Sentences

Answer these questions with complete sentences.

1. Choose one of the following sentences and copy it below.

I like to laugh a lot.
I don't like to laugh.
I sometimes laugh.

_____

_____

2. What things make you laugh (jokes, funny situations, being embarrassed)?

_____

_____

3. When did you laugh last?

_____

_____

4. What happened? Who was with you? Where were you?

_____

_____

5. Did you laugh quietly or loudly?

_____

_____

6. Do you feel like laughing when you think of this situation?

_____

_____

B. Rewrite in Paragraph Form

Rewrite your sentences in the form of a paragraph. Then use the paragraph checklist to check your work.

Paragraph Checklist

- ☐ Did you indent the first line?
- ☐ Did you give your paragraph a title?
- ☐ Did you write the title with a capital letter or letters?
- ☐ Did you put the title in the center at the top of the page?
- ☐ Did you write on every other line?

C. Edit Your Paragraph

Work with a partner or your teacher to edit your sentences. Correct spelling, punctuation, vocabulary, and grammar. Use the editing checklist to help you.

Editing Checklist

- ☐ Subject in every sentence?
- ☐ Verb in every sentence?
- ☐ Words in correct order?
- ☐ Sentences begin with a capital letter?
- ☐ Sentences end with a period directly at the end of a sentence?
- ☐ Sentences have a space between them?
- ☐ Commas in the correct place?
- ☐ Wrong words?
- ☐ Spelling?
- ☐ Missing words (use insertion mark: ^)?

D. Write Your Final Copy

After you edit your paragraph, you can write the final copy.

Weaving It Together

⏱ Timed Writing

Answer these questions with complete sentences. Use capital letters and periods where necessary. You have 50 minutes to answer the questions and rewrite them into paragraph form.

1. How often do you yawn? (every day/sometimes/often/rarely)
2. What makes you yawn? (sleepy/tired/cold/bored)
3. How long does your yawn last?
4. Do you make a noise when you yawn?
5. Do you yawn when somebody else yawns?
6. Are you yawning now?

Connecting to the Internet

A. Use the Internet to research insomnia. Answer the following questions:
   - What are some things that cause insomnia?
   - How many people have insomnia?
   - What happens to people who don't get enough sleep?
   - What are some ways that people try to sleep better?

B. Go to the Internet to find a good Website for jokes and humor. Find a good joke, a funny cartoon, and a riddle. Share them with your classmates.

What Do You Think Now?

Refer to page 51 at the beginning of this unit. Do you know the answers now? Complete the sentence or circle the best answer.

1. Sleep is/is not more important than food.
2. A baby needs _____ hours of sleep a day.
3. Your heartbeat is higher/lower when you laugh.
4. Every minute of laughter is the same as _____ minutes of relaxation.
5. There are/are not laughter clubs where people laugh with no jokes.

Customs

What Do You Think?

Answer the questions with your best guess. Circle **Yes** or **No**.

Do you think . . .

1. a Hindu person has 16 special ceremonies in his or her life?	**Yes**	**No**
2. a Hindu priest names a Hindu baby?	**Yes**	**No**
3. people in Thailand eat with chopsticks?	**Yes**	**No**
4. in Thailand, it is important for a guest to finish his or her rice?	**Yes**	**No**
5. in Thailand, the most important place at a table is at the head, or top, of the table?	**Yes**	**No**

Chapter

7 What to Name the Baby

Pre-Reading

Discuss the answers to these questions with your classmates.

1. What do you see in the picture?
2. What special ceremonies or celebrations does your family have for a baby?
3. In your country, who gives a baby a name and when?

Key Vocabulary

Do you know these words? Match the words or phrases with the meanings.

1. a ceremony _____
2. a priest _____
3. tongue _____
4. a planet _____
5. honey _____
6. a horoscope _____
7. to suggest _____
8. to bless _____

a. a representative of a religion
b. a special event (like a wedding) with special customs
c. sweet liquid made by bees
d. statements about a person's future, made by looking at the stars and planets
e. the organ in your mouth that you speak and taste with
f. a body (like the earth) that moves around a star (like the sun) in space
g. to ask God to make something pure
h. to recommend or advise

Reading

Track 7

What to Name the Baby

1   **A**bout one billion people live in India. Most of these people are Hindu.*
The Hindu religion is also a way of life. In the Hindu religion, there are
special **ceremonies** for important times in a person's life. There are 16
ceremonies in all. For each ceremony there is a special fire, and **priests** say
5   prayers and read from a special book. One of these ceremonies is choosing a
name for a baby.

The birth of a baby is a happy time in a Hindu family. Soon after the
baby is born, the parents wash the baby and write the word *om* on the baby's
tongue. They write the word in **honey** with a pen of gold. *Om* is a special
10   word in the Hindu religion. Hindus say this word over and over again when
they are praying.

Twelve days after the baby is born, a priest visits the family to name the
baby. The priest makes **a horoscope** for the baby. To make this horoscope,
the priest writes down where the stars and **planets** were at the time the baby
15   was born. From this, he reads the baby's future and **suggests** a good name
for the baby. Many children have names of Hindu gods and goddesses or
have names with other religious meanings.

At the ceremony, there are guests. The mother holds the baby. The father is
on one side. In front of them, there is a plate with rice on it. The father uses a
20   long, thin piece of gold to write the name of the family god, the baby's name,
and the date of birth in the rice. Then he says the baby's name in the baby's
right ear. The priest then **blesses** the baby. He also blesses the candies and
food and then passes them to the guests. This ends the ceremony of giving a
name to a baby.

Note: About 83% of the population in India is Hindu.

Vocabulary

A. Vocabulary in Context

Complete these sentences with the words below.

blesses	planets	ceremony
honey	horoscope	priest
suggests	tongue	

1. The Hindus have a _____ to give a name to a baby.
2. The parents write the special word on the baby's _____.
3. They write the word in _____ because most babies like sweet things.
4. A religious man or _____ visits the family 12 days after the baby is born.
5. The priest looks at the positions of the _____ and stars in the sky.
6. He makes a _____ for the new baby from the position of the stars and planets.
7. The priest says what he thinks is a good name. He _____ a name for the baby.
8. At the end of the ceremony, the priest _____ the baby and the food.

Word Partnership	Use **suggest** with:
n.	**analysts** suggest, **experts** suggest, **researchers** suggest, **data** suggest, **findings** suggest, **results** suggest, **studies** suggest, **surveys** suggest

B. Vocabulary in New Context

Answer the questions with complete sentences.

1. What color clothes does a priest in your religion wear?

   Example: In Buddhism, priests wear bright colors.

   _____

   _____

2. What is an important ceremony in a person's life?

_____

_____

3. What is your sign (for your horoscope)?

_____

_____

4. What is the name of a planet?

_____

_____

5. How do you use honey?

_____

_____

6. What can burn or hurt your tongue?

_____

_____

C. Vocabulary Building

Complete these sentences with the words from the box.

suggest (*verb*)	**a suggestion** (*noun*)

1. The priest and not the grandparents will _____ a name for a baby.

2. I agree with your _____. Let's go for a walk.

bless (*verb*)	**a blessing** (*noun*)

3. The priest will _____ the couple at the wedding.

4. The priest gave them _____ before their long and dangerous journey.

pray (verb)	prayers (noun)

5. Every new year, they _____ for a good and lucky year.

6. The priest says _____ for the newborn baby.

Reading Comprehension

A. Looking for the Main Ideas

Answer these questions with complete sentences.

1. What religion has 16 special ceremonies for important times in a person's life?

_____

_____

2. What do Hindu people do after a baby is born?

_____

_____

3. Why does the priest visit the family?

_____

_____

B. Looking for Details

Circle **T** if the sentence is true. Circle **F** if the sentence is false.

1. About a million people live in India.	T	F
2. Most Indians are Hindu.	T	F
3. There are 16 important ceremonies for each Hindu.	T	F
4. Hindu parents write the word *om* in gold on the tongue of their new baby.	T	F
5. At the naming ceremony, there is a plate with rice on it.	T	F
6. The father says the baby's name in the priest's right ear.	T	F

Discussion Questions

Discuss the answers to these questions with your classmates.

1. Do you believe in horoscopes? Why or why not?
2. What is the meaning of your name?
3. Do you like your name? Would you change it?

Critical Thinking Questions

Discuss the answers to these questions with your classmates.

1. How important is a person's name? Do you think a person's name can affect his or her life in any way? How and why?
2. What are some ceremonies that mark special times in life? Why are ceremonies so important to people? What purpose do they serve?

Writing

Writing Skills

A. Count Nouns and Noncount Nouns

Count nouns name things that can be counted. *Noncount nouns* name things that cannot be counted.

When a noun is a count noun:

1. You can put *a* or *an* in front of it.

Example: There is a guest.

2. It has a plural form.

Example: There are guests.

3. You can put a number in front of it.

Example: one guest, two guests

When a noun is a noncount noun:

1. You cannot put *a* or *an* in front of it.

Example: There is milk.

2. It usually does not have a plural form.

Example: There is lots of milk.

3. You cannot put a number in front of it.

Note: You can use *lots of* or *a lot of* before both a count noun and a noncount noun.

There are many noncount nouns in English. Here are some of them. You may add other noncount nouns to the list.

Materials/ Food	Abstract Nouns	Activities/ Subjects	General Nouns
food	luck	dancing	money
fruit	happiness	music	jewelry
gold	love	singing	clothing
hair	fun	homework	furniture
corn	intelligence	grammar	mail
salt	advice	work	cash

Note: *Food*, *fruit*, and *hair* can also be count nouns.

B. Exercises

1. Underline all the noncount nouns in the reading on page 75.

2. Look at the underlined noun in each sentence. Circle **C** if is a count noun. Circle **NC** if it is a noncount noun.

1. Hindu is a religion.	C	NC
2. There is a special fire.	C	NC
3. They write the word *om* on the baby's tongue.	C	NC
4. They write the word in honey.	C	NC
5. The priest visits the family.	C	NC
6. He looks at the stars.	C	NC
7. He makes a horoscope.	C	NC
8. He suggests a name.	C	NC
9. There is a plate.	C	NC
10. The plate has rice on it.	C	NC
11. He uses a piece of gold.	C	NC
12. The priest blesses the food.	C	NC

3. Write *a*, *an*, or *some* in front of each word.

1. We have _____ gift.

2. They have _____ food.

3. She has _____ dollar.

4. He has _____ animal.

5. We see _____ people.

6. They give _____ gold.

7. I listen to _____ music.

8. I have _____ idea.

4. Make sentences using the following words.

1. food

> **Example:** <u>We have a lot of food at the party.</u>

_____

_____

2. money

_____

_____

3. music

_____

_____

4. dancing

_____

_____

5. Find the mistakes. There are 10 mistakes in grammar and capitalization. Find and correct them.

There are about one billions people in india. Most of the people are of the hindu religion. This is the most large religion in asia. It is also the world's older religion. A person cannot become a hindu. You are born hindu or you are not. There are also muslims, christians, and other religions.

Writing Practice

A. Write Sentences

Answer these questions with complete sentences.

1. What is the name of a special day in your country (for example, name day, 16th birthday)?

_____

_____

2. On what date or dates do people celebrate the special day?

_____

_____

3. Is it a religious day or some other kind of day?

_____

_____

4. What do people do on this day?

- Do people wear special clothes?
- Do they have a party at home, or do they go out?
- Do they cook a lot of food?
- Is there music or dancing?
- Do people bring gifts? If so, what kind?

_____

_____

5. Why is this day important?

_____

_____

B. Rewrite in Paragraph Form

Rewrite your sentences in the form of a paragraph. Then use the paragraph checklist to check your work.

Paragraph Checklist

- ☐ Did you indent the first line?
- ☐ Did you give your paragraph a title?
- ☐ Did you write the title with a capital letter or letters?
- ☐ Did you put the title in the center at the top of the page?
- ☐ Did you write on every other line?

C. Edit Your Paragraph

Work with a partner or your teacher to edit your sentences. Correct spelling, punctuation, vocabulary, and grammar. Use the editing checklist to help you.

Editing Checklist

- ☐ Subject in every sentence?
- ☐ Verb in every sentence?
- ☐ Words in correct order?
- ☐ Sentences begin with a capital letter?
- ☐ Sentences end with a period directly at the end of a sentence?
- ☐ Sentences have a space between them?
- ☐ Commas in the correct place?
- ☐ Wrong words?
- ☐ Spelling?
- ☐ Missing words (use insertion mark: ^)?

D. Write Your Final Copy

After you edit your paragraph, you can write the final copy.

Chapter

Eat, Drink, and Know the Customs

Pre-Reading

Discuss the answers to these questions with your classmates.

1. Describe how the people in the picture are eating.
2. In what countries do people not use knives for eating? What do they use?
3. Where does a guest or an important person usually sit at the table in your country?

Key Vocabulary

Do you know these words? Match the words or phrases with the meanings.

1. chopsticks _____
2. a bowl _____
3. to offer _____
4. a host _____
5. to insist _____
6. to refill _____
7. to keep an eye on _____

a. a person who receives guests
b. two thin sticks of wood used to eat food
c. to fill again
d. a deep, round dish, like a dish used for soup
e. to say politely that you are ready to do or give something
f. to watch over
g. to say something strongly

Reading

Track 8

Eat, Drink, and Know the Customs

1   Table customs are different around the world. If you are in Thailand, this information will help you.

    In Thailand, people do not eat with **chopsticks**, like in China, Japan, and Korea. They use spoons and forks. They never use knives. Most food is already

5   cut. If you need to cut things, use the side of your spoon first and then use your fork. The spoon is more important than the fork. If you are right-handed, keep the spoon in your right hand and the fork in your left hand.

    People usually have rice in a separate **bowl**. The rice is not on the same plate with the other food. It is not necessary to finish all your rice or all your

10   food. It is good to leave a little on your plate. If you eat everything, it means you want more.

    People always **offer** you more food. The **host** will ask you two or three times if you want more food. First, you must say no. Then the host insists again, and you must say no again. The host **insists** a third time, and you

15   finally say yes and take a little. If you really don't want any more, take very little and leave it on your plate. It is the same with whatever you are drinking. During the meal, never empty your cup or glass. When it is less than half full, your host or neighbor will **refill** it. Never fill your own glass. Always refill your neighbor's glass. This means that you must **keep an eye on** your

20   neighbor's glass all through the meal.

    The most important place at a table is at the middle. An important guest will sit at the middle of the table on one side, and the host will sit at the middle of the table on the other side. This may be confusing when the table is round, but the Thai get it right somehow.

Vocabulary

A. Vocabulary in Context

Complete these sentences with the words below.

bowl	keep an eye on	chopsticks
offer	host	insist
refill		

1. Chinese people eat their food with _____. The Thai use a spoon and fork.
2. The Thai eat rice in a separate _____.
3. At a dinner, the _____ will seat a guest at the table.
4. The host will _____ you more food.
5. The host will _____ two or three times.
6. You must not _____ your glass or cup. The host or your neighbor will do this.
7. At the table, you must _____ your neighbor's glass and fill it when it is half full.

B. Vocabulary in New Context

Answer these questions with complete sentences.

1. What do you keep an eye on in class?

   Example: _I keep an eye on the clock in class._

   _____

   _____

2. What do you eat in a bowl?

   _____

   _____

3. What do you offer a visitor to your house?

_____

_____

4. In what country do people use chopsticks to eat food?

_____

_____

5. When a guest comes to your house, who is usually the host?

_____

_____

6. When you eat out, what can you refill?

_____

_____

C. Vocabulary Building

Complete these sentences with the correct preposition.

> **More Words That Go Together**
> **keep up** = to continue at the same level
> **keep off** = to stay away from
> **keep down** = to control or prevent

1. Keep _____ the grass!
2. Doctors are trying to keep _____ the epidemic.
3. You are doing very well. Keep _____ the good work!

Now make your own sentences with the words that go together with *keep*.

Reading Comprehension

A. Looking for the Main Ideas

Answer these questions with complete sentences.

1. What do people in Thailand eat with?

_____

_____

2. How many times does the host ask if you want more food?

_____

_____

3. What is the most important place for a guest at a table?

_____

_____

B. Looking for Details

Circle **T** if the sentence is true. Circle **F** if the sentence is false.

1. The Thai generally do not use knives when they eat.   **T**   **F**
2. If you are right-handed, you must keep your fork in your right hand.   **T**   **F**
3. You must always empty your cup or glass.   **T**   **F**
4. You do not fill your own glass.   **T**   **F**
5. If you need to cut food, you use your fork.   **T**   **F**
6. If you do not want more food, you must leave some food on
your plate.   **T**   **F**

Discussion Questions

Discuss the answers to these questions with your classmates.

1. How are table customs in Thailand different from those in your country?

2. How are table customs in the United States different from those in your country?

3. How many kinds of dishes do you usually have at dinner in your country?

4. What is not polite at the table in your country?

Critical Thinking Questions

Discuss the answers to these questions with your classmates.

1. How are table customs changing in our modern world? Do you think it is good for traditional customs to change? Why or why not?

2. Why is it important for a traveler to know the customs in the country he or she is visiting? What can happen if a traveler doesn't know the customs? What happens when the traveler does know the customs?

Writing

Writing Skills

A. Prepositional Phrases

A *phrase* is a group of words. A *prepositional phrase* begins with a preposition. The preposition always has an object. The *object of a preposition* can be a noun or a pronoun.

Examples:

The Thai do not eat   <u>with</u>   <u>chopsticks</u>.
                      (preposition)   (object of preposition)

Keep the spoon   <u>in</u>   <u>your right hand</u>.
                (preposition)   (object of preposition)

Sometimes there is more than one prepositional phrase in a sentence.

Example:

The rice is not   <u>on the same plate</u>   <u>with your food</u>.
         (prepositional phrase)   (prepositional phrase)

Sometimes a prepositional phrase comes at the beginning of a sentence.

Example:

<u>During the meal,</u>   drink so that your cup is never empty.
(prepositional phrase)

The following are some common prepositions:

about	at	down	of	to
above	before	during	on	under
across	behind	for	out	until
after	below	from	over	up
against	beside	in	since	with
among	between	into	through	without
around	by	near	till	

B. Exercises

1. Underline the prepositional phrase (PP) in these sentences.

   1. Use the side <u>of your spoon</u>.
                      PP
   2. Table customs are different around the world.
   3. Keep the fork in your left hand.
   4. People usually serve rice in a separate bowl.
   5. The most important place at a table is at the middle.
   6. It is good to leave a little food on your plate.

2. Complete these sentences with the correct preposition.

   1. The Thai usually have dinner _____ six in the evening.
   2. We eat _____ a knife and fork.
   3. We put soup _____ a bowl.
   4. We usually drink tea _____ the end of the meal.
   5. We have dinner _____ the dining room.
   6. In my country, it is not polite to eat _____ your fingers.

3. Find the mistakes. There are 10 mistakes in grammar and punctuation. Find and correct them.

   Thai food is deliciously. They eat a lot of vegetable, seafood, rices, and noodle. When you eat Thai food it is usually spicy. They usually have breakfast from 7:30 to 9 at the morning. They have tea and rices. They drink tea without sugars, milks, or lemon. The Thai do not eat cheeses.

Writing Practice

A. Write Sentences

Answer these questions with complete sentences.

1. What time do people in your country usually have dinner?

_____

_____

2. What is on the table (bowls, glasses, cups, different kinds of food, bread, rice)?

_____

_____

3. What does each person have (a bowl, a plate, a napkin)?

_____

_____

4. What do you eat with?

_____

_____

5. What do you eat?

_____

_____

6. What is not polite at the table in your country?

_____

_____

B. Rewrite in Paragraph Form

Rewrite your sentences in the form of a paragraph. Then use the paragraph checklist to check your work.

Paragraph Checklist

☐ Did you indent the first line?
☐ Did you give your paragraph a title?
☐ Did you write the title with a capital letter or letters?
☐ Did you put the title in the center at the top of the page?
☐ Did you write on every other line?

C. Edit Your Paragraph

Work with a partner or your teacher to edit your sentences. Correct spelling, punctuation, vocabulary, and grammar. Use the editing checklist to help you.

Editing Checklist

☐ Subject in every sentence?
☐ Verb in every sentence?
☐ Words in correct order?
☐ Sentences begin with a capital letter?
☐ Sentences end with a period directly at the end of a sentence?
☐ Sentences have a space between them?
☐ Commas in the correct place?
☐ Wrong words?
☐ Spelling?
☐ Missing words (use insertion mark: ^)?

D. Write Your Final Copy

After you edit your paragraph, you can write the final copy.

Weaving It Together

⏱ Timed Writing

Answer these questions with complete sentences. Use capital letters and periods where necessary. You have 50 minutes to answer the questions and rewrite them into paragraph form. Start your paragraph with these words: "In my country, when a person invites you to their home for the first time for dinner at 8:00, there are some things you do. It is the custom." Now answer the questions:

1. Do you arrive on time (8:00), early, or a little late?
2. Do you usually take a gift with you?
3. What kind of gifts do you usually take?
4. Do you usually say something nice about the house or the dinner table?
5. When you eat dinner, do you finish all the food on your plate? Do you ask for more?
6. What do you say at the end of the meal?
7. When do you leave?

Connecting to the Internet

A. What does your name mean? Go to the Internet to find a Website that tells you the meaning of your name. Then find the 10 most popular baby names last year for boys and girls. Find the meanings of these names.

B. Use the Internet to research table customs in Ethiopia, Bangladesh, Vietnam, and England. Which Websites were the most helpful? How are the customs in these countries similar to or different from your country?

What Do You Think Now?

Refer to page 73 at the beginning of this unit. Do you know the answers now? Complete the sentence, or circle the best answer.

1. A Hindu person has _____ special ceremonies in his or her life.
2. A Hindu priest names/does not name a Hindu baby.
3. People in Thailand eat with _____.
4. In Thailand, it is important for a guest to finish/not to finish his or her rice.
5. In Thailand, the most important place at a table is at the _____ of the table.

Food

UNIT 5

What Do You Think?

Answer the questions with your best guess. Circle **Yes** or **No**.

Do you think . . .

1. chocolate was a drink in the beginning?	**Yes**	**No**
2. Americans made the first chocolate bar?	**Yes**	**No**
3. the world's most popular drink is tea?	**Yes**	**No**
4. coffee first started in Ethiopia?	**Yes**	**No**
5. Americans drink the most coffee in the world?	**Yes**	**No**

Chapter

 **9**

For the Love of Chocolate

Pre-Reading

Discuss the answers to these questions with your classmates.

1. How often do you eat chocolate?
2. What kinds of foods can have chocolate in them?
3. Do you think chocolate is good for you?

Key Vocabulary

Do you know these words? Match the words or phrases with the meanings.

1. hot _____
2. bitter _____
3. to add _____
4. instead of _____
5. a chocolate bar _____
6. energy _____
7. a chemical _____

a. in place of
b. making your mouth burn from the pepper
c. having a strong taste, like coffee with no sugar
d. a piece of chocolate in the shape of a rectangle
e. the power to be active and work and play
f. something that works by chemistry to have a special effect, often on the body
g. to put together with something else

Reading

For the Love of Chocolate

Track 9

1   The Aztecs of Mexico knew about chocolate a long time ago. They made it into a drink. Sometimes they put **hot** chili peppers with the chocolate. They called the drink *xocoatl*, which means "**bitter** juice." This is where the word *chocolate* comes from.

5   The Spanish went to Mexico and took the drink from the land of the Aztecs back to Spain. The Spanish didn't like peppers, so they **added** sugar. They also liked to drink chocolate hot, and hot chocolate was born. This drink became very popular in Europe. People added different things like eggs to the chocolate drink. But everybody's favorite was chocolate in milk **instead of** water.

10   There was still no hard chocolate until around 1850. Then the British made the first **chocolate bar**. Twenty-five years later, two men in Switzerland mixed milk with the hard chocolate. Milk chocolate soon became a favorite all over the world.

Is chocolate good for you? For hundreds of years, people thought that
15   chocolate was good for health. Doctors told people to have a chocolate drink for headaches and many other problems. Today, there is good news for chocolate lovers. Scientists think that a little bit of chocolate is good for you! It gives you **energy** and has vitamins to keep your body healthy.

The Aztecs believed that chocolate made you intelligent. Today, we do not
20   believe this. But chocolate has a special **chemical** called phenylethylamine. This is the same chemical the body makes when a person is in love. Which do you prefer—eating chocolate or being in love?

Vocabulary

A. Vocabulary in Context

Circle the letter of the best answer.

1. The Aztecs liked _____ food like chili peppers.
   a. hot   b. hard

2. The Aztecs drank _____ chocolate.
   a. bitter   b. sweet

3. The Spanish _____ sugar to the chocolate drink.
   a. called   b. added

4. People liked to use milk _____ water for a chocolate drink.
   a. with   b. instead of

5. The first hard chocolate was a British _____.
   a. chocolate bit   b. chocolate bar

6. Chocolate is good for the body. It gives people _____.
   a. energy   b. intelligence

7. Chocolate has phenylethylamine. This is a _____.
   a. vitamin   b. chemical

Word Partnership	Use **energy** with:
adj.	**full of** energy, **physical** energy, **atomic** energy, **nuclear** energy, **solar** energy
v.	**focus** energy, **conserve/save** energy

B. Vocabulary in New Context

Answer the questions with complete sentences.

1. Let's say you can't eat chocolate. What do you eat instead of chocolate?

   Example: _Instead of chocolate, I eat fruit._

   _____

   _____

2. What is the name of your favorite chocolate bar?

_____

_____

3. What food or drink gives you energy?

_____

_____

4. What is something that is bitter?

_____

_____

5. What do you add to food to make it sweet?

_____

_____

6. What do you add to food to make it hot?

_____

_____

C. Vocabulary Building

Complete these sentences with the words from the box.

add (*verb*)	**(an) addition** (*noun*)

1. When you _____ 8 to 7 you get 15.
2. We have _____ to our family: a baby boy.

energize (*verb*)	**energy** (*noun*)

3. My five-year-old sister has a lot of _____.
4. Every week he gives a talk to _____ his workers.

hot (*adjective*)	**heat** (*noun*)

5. We are having very _____ weather at the moment.

6. The _____ of my body melted the chocolate in my pocket.

Reading Comprehension

A. Looking for the Main Ideas

Circle the letter of the best answer.

1. The Aztecs made _____.
   a. chili peppers into a drink
   b. chocolate into a drink
   c. chocolate peppers

2. The Spanish _____.
   a. were the first to know about chocolate
   b. gave chocolate to the Aztecs
   c. took the chocolate drink to Europe

3. Chocolate _____.
   a. has a special chemical
   b. has no special chemicals
   c. makes you love chemicals

B. Looking for Details

Circle **T** if the sentence is true. Circle **F** if the sentence is false.

1. The Aztecs put sugar into chocolate.	T	F
2. The word *chocolate* means "bitter juice."	T	F
3. The Spanish took peppers to Europe.	T	F
4. In 1850, people began to eat chocolate.	T	F
5. Switzerland made the first milk chocolate.	T	F
6. Chocolate has vitamins.	T	F

Discussion Questions

Discuss the answers to these questions with your classmates.

1. Why do you think people like chocolate?
2. What is the most popular kind of chocolate in your country?
3. The Aztecs drank chocolate with spices like vanilla or chili peppers. What other kinds of things can you mix with chocolate?
4. How would you create a wonderful chocolate dish?

Critical Thinking Questions

Discuss the answers to these questions with your classmates.

1. Some people are addicted to chocolate. That means they can't stop eating it. Are there foods that you are addicted to? Why is it so difficult to stop eating things we like? How can being addicted to certain foods harm people? Can it ever help?
2. Some foods are called "comfort foods." That means they make people feel good. They make people remember their home. What foods are comfort foods for you? Are comfort foods always good for people? Why or why not?

Writing

Writing Skills

A. Writing Instructions

When you write instructions, you must use exact words to describe each step. It is also important to give all the steps in the correct order.

B. Exercises

1. Look at these pictures. Number them in the correct order. Then fill in the blanks with the words from the box.

~~Fill~~	Put	Pour	Leave	Boil

_____

_____ for a few minutes.

_____ the tea into the cup.

_____ some tea into the teapot.

____1____

Fill _____ the kettle with water.

_____

_____ the water.

_____ the teapot with boiling water.

Now write the complete sentences in the correct order.

1. _____

2. _____

3. _____

4. _____

5. _____

6. _____

2. Write six sentences to show how you make coffee or chocolate.

1. _____

_____

2. _____

_____

3. _____

_____

4. _____

_____

5. _____

_____

6. _____

_____

3. Find the mistakes. There are 10 mistakes in grammar and capitalization. Find and correct them.

Jackie loves chocolates. When she has money, she buy a box of belgian chocolates. They are the most expensivest chocolates. She like chocolates bitter. She doesn't like the swiss chocolates milk. When she is sadly, she eats one piece of chocolate. When she is tired, she eats one. After she eat a chocolate, jackie is Happy.

Writing Practice

A. Write Sentences

Answer these questions with complete sentences.

1. Which do you like best: ice cream, cookies, cake, or chocolate?

_____

_____

2. Do you eat this food every day? How many times a week or month do you eat it?

_____

_____

3. When do you eat it (when you are very hungry, when you are sad, on a special day)?

_____

_____

4. What do you eat it with (milk, coffee, alone)? Do you eat it after a meal or between meals?

_____

_____

5. How much do you like this food?

_____

_____

B. Rewrite in Paragraph Form

Rewrite your sentences in the form of a paragraph. Then use the paragraph checklist to check your work.

Paragraph Checklist

- ☐ Did you indent the first line?
- ☐ Did you give your paragraph a title?
- ☐ Did you write the title with a capital letter or letters?
- ☐ Did you put the title in the center at the top of the page?
- ☐ Did you write on every other line?

C. Edit Your Paragraph

Work with a partner or your teacher to edit your sentences. Correct spelling, punctuation, vocabulary, and grammar. Use the editing checklist to help you.

Editing Checklist

- ☐ Subject in every sentence?
- ☐ Verb in every sentence?
- ☐ Words in correct order?
- ☐ Sentences begin with a capital letter?
- ☐ Sentences end with a period directly at the end of a sentence?
- ☐ Sentences have a space between them?
- ☐ Commas in the correct place?
- ☐ Wrong words?
- ☐ Spelling?
- ☐ Missing words (use insertion mark: ^)?

D. Write Your Final Copy

After you edit your paragraph, you can write the final copy.

Chapter 10 Coffee: The World's Most Popular Drink

Pre-Reading

Discuss the answers to these questions with your classmates.

1. Why do you like or not like coffee?
2. What kinds of coffee are there?
3. How do you like to drink your coffee?

Key Vocabulary

Do you know these words? Match the words or phrases with the meanings.

1. beans _____
2. to take care of _____
3. to boil _____
4. too _____
5. liquid _____
6. to discover _____
7. excited _____

a. to heat until it begins to bubble
b. to find something that nobody knew about before you
c. anything that runs or flows like water
d. the seeds of a plant
e. having strong feelings or lots of energy
f. to look after
g. also

Reading

Coffee: The World's Most Popular Drink

Track 10

1   **P**eople all over the world drink coffee. It is the world's most popular drink. The French call it *café*, the Germans *Kaffee*, the Japanese *koohi*, the Turkish *kahve*. But the people of Sweden drink the most coffee—more than five cups a day. Over half of American adults drink it every day, but not as much as in
5   Sweden. Too much coffee is bad for your health.

We don't know who really **discovered** coffee. There is a popular story about a young man who discovered coffee in Ethiopia, a country in Africa. Around the year 700, there was a young man called Kaldi who **took care of** goats. One day, he watched them while they were eating some plants. Soon
10 after they ate the plants, the goats became very **excited**, and they did not sleep that night. Kaldi tried the plants himself, and he became very excited, **too**. Other people tried the plants. They decided to **boil** the plants and then drink the **liquid**. They too couldn't sleep well at night. This drink became popular and went from Ethiopia to Arabia. By 1200, it was a popular drink
15 in the Arab world. The word *coffee* comes from the Arab word *qahwah*. Coffee then traveled from Arabia to Turkey, Europe, and the rest of the world.

Coffee has been very popular in history. Many famous people loved coffee. The French writer Voltaire needed 72 cups every day. In 1735, the German musician Johann Sebastian Bach wrote music about coffee. Another German
20 musician, Beethoven, counted 60 **beans** for each cup of coffee he made. That was strong!

There are coffee houses and coffee bars all over North America today. There are bars with all kinds of coffee. There are different sizes and flavors. There are bars where you can use the Internet while you drink your coffee!

Vocabulary

A. Vocabulary in Context

Complete these sentences. Circle the letter of the best answer.

1. A young man called Kaldi _____ coffee in Ethiopia.
   a. discovered   b. grew

2. Kaldi _____ goats.
   a. took care of   b. discovered

3. When the goats ate the coffee plants, the goats became _____.
   a. popular   b. excited

4. Other people ate the plants, and they became excited _____.
   a. too   b. much

5. Some people count how many _____ they want in their coffee.
   a. cups   b. beans

6. People started to _____ the coffee plants in water.
   a. boil   b. use

7. Then they drank the _____.
   a. liquid   b. flavors

B. Vocabulary in New Context

Choose the best answer. Then use the answer in a complete sentence.

1. Which of the following can make a person excited?
   going to sleep   doing homework   watching a movie

Example: Watching a movie can make a person excited.

2. Which of the following do we usually boil?
   a tomato   a potato   an orange

3. Which of the following discovered America?
   Christopher Columbus   George Washington   Mahatma Gandhi

4. Which of the following do we usually take care of?

a teacher   a baby   a country

C. Vocabulary Building

Complete these sentences with the words from the box.

discover (*verb*)	**discovery** (*noun*)

1. Scientists are trying to _____ a cure for cancer.

2. The _____ of penicillin saved many lives.

excited (*verb*)	**excitement** (*noun*)

3. The music at the concert _____ the audience.

4. There is _____ everywhere just before the clock strikes midnight on New Year's Day.

liquefy (*verb*)	**liquid** (*noun*)

5. To _____ butter, you heat it.

6. You must drink a lot of _____ when you have a cold.

Reading Comprehension

A. Looking for the Main Ideas

Circle the letter of the best answer.

1. Coffee is _____.
   a. popular only in America
   b. the world's most popular drink
   c. bad for your health

2. A story says _____.
   a. a young man discovered coffee in Ethiopia
   b. people discovered coffee in Arabia
   c. goats discovered coffee in Turkey

3. Coffee _____.
   a. has not been popular in history
   b. has been popular in history with musicians
   c. has been popular in history

B. Looking for Details

Circle **T** if the sentence is true. Circle **F** if the sentence is false.

1. The people of Sweden drink five cups of coffee a day.		**T**	**F**
2. Coffee went from Ethiopia to Turkey.		**T**	**F**
3. The word *coffee* comes from a Turkish word.		**T**	**F**
4. The Turkish name for coffee is *kahve*.		**T**	**F**
5. Coffee was popular in Arabia first, then in Europe.		**T**	**F**
6. Voltaire drank 60 cups of coffee every day.		**T**	**F**

Discussion Questions

Discuss the answers to these questions with your classmates.

1. What is the most popular drink in your country?
2. What is your favorite drink?
3. Which drink do you not like? Why?

Critical Thinking Questions

Discuss the answers to these questions with your classmates.

1. Do you go to coffee houses or bars? Why or why not? Why are coffee houses so popular? Other than coffee, what do they provide for people? Are there other kinds of places that serve a similar purpose?
2. Drinking too much coffee is bad for one's health. What other drinks or foods are bad for your health if you have too much of them? Why do people do things that aren't good for them?

Writing

Writing Skills

A. The Pronouns *it* and *them*

It is a pronoun. A *pronoun* replaces another word so that you do not repeat the same word too many times.

Use the pronoun **it** for singular words. Use the pronoun **them** for plural words.

Example:

Kaldi took care of his goats. He watched **them** while they were eating some plants.

B. Exercises

1. Look back to the reading about coffee on page 110.

    1. Underline the pronoun **it** in the first paragraph.
    2. How many times do you see the pronoun **it**?
    3. What does the pronoun **it** replace?

2. Replace the repeated word with the correct pronoun.

    1. Jack loves coffee. He drinks coffee every morning.

    _____

    _____

    2. I can't drink coffee at night. Coffee keeps me awake.

    _____

    _____

3. I usually have coffee with milk, but sometimes I have coffee with cream.

_____

_____

4. At 4 every day, my friend eats cookies. She likes to eat cookies with a cup of coffee.

_____

_____

3. Find the mistakes. There are 10 mistakes in grammar, punctuation, and capitalization. Find and correct them.

Tony always drink hotly coffee. He drinks it with milk, but no sugars. He doesn't like coffee strong like turkish coffee. His Favorite is brazilian Coffee. He drinks four smalls cups every day. He has a cup for breakfast and a cup at 11 O'clock. After lunch, he has a cup. When he gets home from work he has a cup.

Writing Practice

A. Write Sentences

Answer these questions with complete sentences.

1. What is your favorite drink (tea, coffee, hot chocolate, milk, soda)?

_____

_____

2. How do you drink it (in a cup, in a glass, in a bowl, with sugar)?

_____

_____

3. When do you drink it (at breakfast, at meal times, between meals)?

_____

_____

4. How many cups do you drink a day?

_____

_____

5. How much do you like this drink? Can you live without it?

_____

_____

B. Rewrite in Paragraph Form

Rewrite your sentences in the form of a paragraph. Then use the paragraph checklist to check your work.

Paragraph Checklist

☐ Did you indent the first line?
☐ Did you give your paragraph a title?
☐ Did you write the title with a capital letter or letters?
☐ Did you put the title in the center at the top of the page?
☐ Did you write on every other line?

C. Edit Your Paragraph

Work with a partner or your teacher to edit your sentences. Correct spelling, punctuation, vocabulary, and grammar. Use the editing checklist to help you.

Editing Checklist

- ☐ Subject in every sentence?
- ☐ Verb in every sentence?
- ☐ Words in correct order?
- ☐ Sentences begin with a capital letter?
- ☐ Sentences end with a period directly at the end of a sentence?
- ☐ Sentences have a space between them?
- ☐ Commas in the correct place?
- ☐ Wrong words?
- ☐ Spelling?
- ☐ Missing words (use insertion mark: ^)?

D. Write Your Final Copy

After you edit your paragraph, you can write the final copy.

Weaving It Together

⏱ Timed Writing

Answer these questions with complete sentences. Use capital letters and periods where necessary. You have 50 minutes to answer the questions and rewrite them into paragraph form.

1. Which do you like best: potatoes or rice?
2. Do you eat this food every day? How many times a week or month do you eat it?
3. When do you eat it?
4. How do you eat it (boiled/steamed/fried, etc.)?
5. What food do you eat with it?
6. Is this an important food for you?

Connecting to the Internet

A. Which countries produce coffee and chocolate? Go to the Internet to find out where these foods are grown. Then find out which two countries drink the most coffee and which two eat the most chocolate.

B. Use the Internet to research the following foods and drinks: ginger ale, spaghetti, hot dog, hamburger, croissant, chewing gum. Write the country of origin next to each food. Then answer these questions:
   • Which food or drink has the most interesting history to you?
   • Which history surprised you the most?
   • Which food do you like to eat the most?
   • Which food don't you like?

What Do You Think Now?

Refer to page 97 at the beginning of this unit. Do you know the answers now? Complete the sentence, or circle the best answer.

1. Chocolate was/was not a drink in the beginning.
2. _____ made the first chocolate bar.
3. The world's most popular drink is _____.
4. Coffee first started/did not start in Ethiopia.
5. _____ drink the most coffee in the world.

Inventions

UNIT **6**

What Do You Think?

Answer the questions with your best guess. Circle **Yes** or **No**.

Do you think . . .

1. people in England saw frozen food in packages for the first time?	**Yes**	**No**
2. people didn't like frozen food in packages at first?	**Yes**	**No**
3. Birdseye is the name of the person who started a company?	**Yes**	**No**
4. Gillette invented a razor that you could throw away?	**Yes**	**No**
5. Gillette had his picture on every package of razors?	**Yes**	**No**

Chapter 11

Dinner Fresh from the Freezer

Pre-Reading

Discuss the answers to these questions with your classmates.

1. Which of the foods on the table can come from your freezer?
2. Does frozen food and fresh food have the same taste?
3. Which foods can be frozen?

Key Vocabulary

Do you know these words? Match the words or phrases with the meanings.

1. convenient _____
2. curiosity _____
3. delicious _____
4. diet _____
5. fur _____
6. frozen food _____
7. taste _____
8. try out _____

a. food that is hard because it is stored at a very cold temperature
b. tasty
c. interest
d. helpful; useful
e. see if something works or not
f. flavor
g. thick hair of animals
h. the kind of food you eat every day

Reading

Track 11

Dinner Fresh from the Freezer

1   **Y**ou need to make dinner, but don't have any fresh vegetables. So you go to the freezer and take out some frozen ones. When you have dinner, the **taste** of the vegetables is fresh and **delicious**. You can thank Clarence Birdseye for that. Clarence Birdseye invented a way for us to have **frozen**
5   **food** in **convenient** packages.

Clarence Birdseye was born in 1886 in Brooklyn, New York. He was one of eight children. He loved nature and animals. Later, he started to study biology at college. He didn't finish college and started to work to make money. In many jobs around the country, he worked with animals and nature.

10   In 1912, Birdseye went to the north of Canada. He liked it there and bought and sold **fur**. He also took his new wife and baby son there. They lived in a cabin 250 miles away from the nearest doctor. He often traveled with the local Inuit[1] people, and he went fishing with them. As soon as one of them caught a fish, it quickly froze because the air was so cold. He asked them, "Are
15   we going to eat this fish today?" The Inuit replied, "No, we already have fish for one month." Birdseye didn't understand. How could fish stay for a month and not go bad? Later, when he ate the frozen fish, it was as delicious as the fresh fish. Then he got the idea! When you freeze fish fast enough, it doesn't change its taste or the way it looks. He tried this new idea on vegetables. He
20   froze cabbage so his family could eat vegetables in the winter.

In 1917, he returned to the United States and took different jobs. In the end, he worked for a fish company and started to **try out** the quick-freezing method he learned in Canada. Finally, in 1924, he started a company called Birdseye Seafoods. It sold frozen foods such as fish, meat, and vegetables. In 1930, he
25   tested the foods in Springfield, Massachusetts. For the first time, shoppers saw frozen foods in their grocery store. Did they buy them? Yes, they did! And what a change Birdseye made to the American **diet**, all because of his **curiosity**.

---

[1]**Inuit:** native people who live in the north of Canada, Alaska, Greenland, and Siberia. These people were called Eskimos before.

Vocabulary

A. Vocabulary in Context

Complete these sentences with the words below.

convenient	diet	taste
curiosity	fur	try out
delicious	frozen food	

1. Today we often have _____ when we cannot have fresh food.
2. In Canada, Birdseye sold the thick hair on animals, or _____, for money.
3. To have frozen food in a package, ready to use whenever you want, is _____.
4. After you cook frozen vegetables, the _____ is like fresh vegetables.
5. The meal had frozen vegetables, but it was good and _____.
6. The American _____ changed because of Birdseye's frozen foods.
7. When Birdseye came back to the United States, he started to _____ what he learned in Canada.
8. Birdseye's _____ made a change to the American way of eating.

Word Partnership	Use **diet** with:
adj.	**balanced** diet, **healthy** diet, **proper** diet, **strict** diet
n.	diet **and exercise**, diet **supplements**, diet **pills**
prep.	**on a** diet

B. Vocabulary in New Context

Answer the questions with complete sentences.

1. Which food is delicious to you?

   Example: _Chocolate cake with ice cream is delicious to me._

   _____

   _____

2. What do you usually put on food to give it taste?

_____

_____

3. What machine in your home is the most convenient for you?

_____

_____

4. Do you eat frozen food? If yes, say what frozen food (pizza, peas, fish, etc.)

_____

_____

5. What is a popular food in the American diet?

_____

_____

C. Vocabulary Building

Complete these sentences with the words from the box.

convenient (_adjective_)	**convenience** (_noun_)

1. Today many people use a microwave oven for _____.
2. A washing machine at home is _____.

tasty (_adjective_)	**taste** (_verb_)

3. I have a cold so I can't _____ anything.
4. This soup is good. It's _____.

curious (_adjective_)	**curiosity** (_noun_)

5. My brother has a _____ about machines and how they work.
6. My grandmother is always _____ about what her neighbors are doing.

Reading Comprehension

A. Looking for the Main Ideas

Circle the letter of the best answer.

1. Birdseye always loved _____.
   a. animals and nature
   b. fishing
   c. money

2. Birdseye got the idea of frozen food _____.
   a. because it was cold in Canada
   b. from the Inuit in Canada
   c. from frozen cabbages

3. Birdseye changed _____.
   a. the taste of American food
   b. American frozen foods
   c. the American way of eating

B. Looking for Details

Circle **T** if the sentence is true. Circle **F** if the sentence is false.

1. Clarence Birdseye studied biology in college.	T	F
2. Birdseye liked Canada.	T	F
3. Birdseye had eight children.	T	F
4. Birdseye went fishing with the Inuit.	T	F
5. Birdseye had a company called Birdseye Frozen Foods.	T	F
6. Shoppers saw frozen foods for the first time in 1924.	T	F

Discussion Questions

Discuss the answers to these questions with your classmates.

1. How did Birdseye's invention change the American diet and lifestyle? Name some changes.
2. What other inventions have changed the way we eat in the modern world?
3. What changes in food, diet, and eating habits do you think we'll see in the future?

Critical Thinking Questions

Discuss the answers to these questions with your classmates.

1. What are some of the good points and bad points of fast food and frozen meals?
2. Do you think people in America eat healthy food? What is your idea of healthy food?

Writing

Writing Skills

A. Comparing Things with *as . . . as*

When you compare two things that are the same, use:

as + adjective + as

Examples:

Frozen vegetables can be **as tasty as** fresh vegetables.

Frozen pizzas are **as big as** fresh pizzas.

For the negative form, use:

not as + adjective + as

Examples:

A microwave is **not as big as** a refrigerator.

Frozen peas are **not as expensive as** fresh peas.

B. Exercises

1. Make sentences with the words below and a form of the verb *to be*.

When you see the = symbol, use **as . . . as**.
When you see the < symbol, use **not as . . . as**.

1. Frozen peas = fresh peas (tasty)

Example: Frozen peas are as tasty as fresh peas.

2. fast food < fresh food (healthy)

_____

_____

3. fresh food < fast food (popular)

_____

_____

4. fast food < fresh food (expensive)

_____

_____

5. frozen dessert = fresh dessert (good)

_____

_____

6. frozen fish = fresh fish (well-liked)

_____

_____

2. Work alone, with a partner, or in a group. Make sentences with the comparative. Use **as . . . as, –er . . . than,** or **more . . . than**.

1. a refrigerator/a microwave oven (big)

_____

_____

2. a refrigerator/a microwave oven (expensive)

_____

_____

3. a microwave oven/a freezer (important)

_____

_____

3. Find the mistakes. There are 10 mistakes in grammar and capitalization. Find and correct them.

    We often called a refrigerator a "fridge." She is a very convenience appliance in our homes. The Refrigerator for the home start around 1850. Before the refrigerator, people used ices to keep food cool. They bought ices and put the ices in Iceboxes. They like their iceboxes, and didn't want to buy refrigerators!

Writing Practice

A. Write Sentences

Answer these questions with complete sentences.

1. Do you think the microwave is a convenient invention?

_____

_____

2. Do you think many modern homes have one?

_____

_____

3. What kinds of foods do you use a microwave oven for?

_____

_____

4. How is this invention better than a normal oven?

_____

_____

5. Do you or someone you know use a microwave oven?

_____

_____

6. Do you think more people will have a microwave in their kitchen?

_____

_____

B. Rewrite in Paragraph Form

Rewrite your sentences in the form of a paragraph. Then use the paragraph checklist to check your work.

Paragraph Checklist

- ☐ Did you indent the first line?
- ☐ Did you give your paragraph a title?
- ☐ Did you write the title with a capital letter or letters?
- ☐ Did you put the title in the center at the top of the page?
- ☐ Did you write on every other line?

C. Edit Your Paragraph

Work with a partner or your teacher to edit your sentences. Correct spelling, punctuation, vocabulary, and grammar. Use the editing checklist to help you.

Editing Checklist

- ☐ Subject in every sentence?
- ☐ Verb in every sentence?
- ☐ Words in correct order?
- ☐ Sentences begin with a capital letter?
- ☐ Sentences end with a period directly at the end of a sentence?
- ☐ Sentences have a space between them?
- ☐ Commas in the correct place?
- ☐ Wrong words?
- ☐ Spelling?
- ☐ Missing words (use insertion mark: ^)?

D. Write Your Final Copy

After you edit your paragraph, you can write the final copy.

Chapter

12 A Sharp Idea from King Gillette

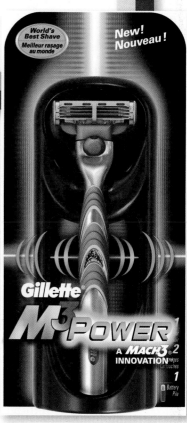

Pre-Reading

Discuss the answers to these questions with your classmates.

1. What kind of razors do you see in the photos?
2. What type of razor do you like?
3. Why do you like this type of razor?

Key Vocabulary

Do you know these words? Match the words or phrases with the meanings.

1. blade _____
2. disposable _____
3. dull _____
4. encouraged _____
5. household name _____
6. invention _____
7. product _____
8. sharpen _____

a. something you use and then throw away
b. persuaded someone to do something
c. the cutting part of a knife or razor
d. something that is created for the first time; a discovery
e. not sharp
f. to make sharp so it cuts easily
g. something that is famous or known by many people
h. something made to be sold; merchandise

Reading

A Sharp Idea from King Gillette

Track 12

1   A salesman named King Camp Gillette invented a **disposable** razor. His **invention** became a **household name**. It changed the way people shave all over the world to this day.

King Camp Gillette was born in a small town in the state of Wisconsin
5   in the USA. When he was young, the family moved to Chicago. The family worked hard. His father worked at various inventions. Gillette always liked the idea of inventing something, too. At 18, he left school and worked as a salesman.

By age 40, Gillette was still a salesman. Both his parents were more
10   successful than he was. His mother published the famous *White House Cookbook*, and his father had his own few inventions. The younger Gillette worked hard and also wanted to be an inventor. The president of the company he worked for **encouraged** him. He told him to invent something people could use and throw away. Gillette often thought about this.

15   One day when he was ready to shave, his razor was too **dull**. It didn't cut. He thought, "I just spend so much time sharpening this **blade**. Then when I **sharpen** it, it's too sharp and I cut myself." He decided, "I'll make a razor with a safe, removable blade. When the blade is dull, you can throw it away and buy another blade."

20   Gillette started to work on this idea. Another inventor named William Emery Nickerson helped him. They became partners. Five years later, they started a company called the American Safety Razor Company. A year later, Gillette renamed the company to Gillette Safety Razor Company. In 1903, he sold 51 razors and 68 blades. The next year he sold 90,884 razors and 123,648
25   blades. This was because Gillette had a good product and a good idea. He knew how to advertise. He gave away razors for free to sell more blades. Other companies tried to copy his **product**, but Gillette became the most popular company. By age 55, Gillette was a millionaire. He was famous, too, because his picture was on every package of razor blades. People all over the world

30 asked for razors with the picture of a man on them. Gillette once said, "In my travels, I have found it in the most northern town of Norway and in the heart of the Sahara Desert." Sadly, in 1926, the stock market crashed[1] and Gillette lost all his money.

---

[1]**stock market crashed:** people lost all the money they had in stocks and shares in the stock market

Vocabulary

A. Vocabulary in Context

Complete these sentences with the words and phrases below.

blade	encouraged	product
disposable	household name	sharpen
dull	invention	

1. Everybody knows the name Gillette. It is a _____.

2. When a knife or razor doesn't cut, it is _____.

3. The part of a knife or razor that cuts is the _____.

4. Gillette's _____ changed the way people shave.

5. The president of the company Gillette worked for _____ him to invent.

6. Gillette invented a _____ razor, or a razor you can throw away.

7. Gillette's new _____ did not sell well the first year.

8. With the old razors, you had to _____ the blade when it didn't cut anymore.

B. Vocabulary in New Context

Answer the questions with complete sentences.

1. What is a disposable product?

Example: *Paper tissues like Kleenex are disposable.*

_____

_____

2. What is a household name?

_____

_____

3. Knives and razors have blades. What else has a blade or blades?

_____

_____

4. What is something you sharpen?

_____

_____

5. What product do you buy to wash your hair?

_____

_____

6. What is the invention you use the most?

_____

_____

C. Vocabulary Building

Complete these sentences with the words from the box.

invent (*verb*)	**invention** (*noun*)

1. Alexander Graham Bell had the idea to _____ the telephone.

2. The _____ of electricity has changed our lives.

encourage (*verb*)	**encouragement** (*noun*)

3. I always _____ her to continue with her studies and finish medical school.

4. We know it is difficult, so we give him a lot of _____ to continue.

produce (*verb*)	product (*noun*)

5. There is always a new electronic _____ on the market.

6. The company has started to _____ a very light and cheap razor now.

Reading Comprehension

A. Looking for the Main Ideas

Answer the questions with complete sentences.

1. When Gillette was a salesman, what did he really want to do?

_____

_____

2. What kind of razor did Gillette want to make?

_____

_____

3. Why did Gillette sell so many razors?

_____

_____

B. Looking for Details

One word in each sentence is not correct. Rewrite the sentences with the correct word.

1. At 18, he left school and worked as a writer.

_____

_____

2. The company president told Gillette to invent something people could use and put away.

_____

_____

3. One day when he was ready to shave, his razor was too sharp.

_____

_____

4. King Gillette and William Nickerson started a company called the Gillette Safety Razor Company.

_____

_____

5. Gillette gave away blades for free.

_____

_____

6. He was famous because his name was on every package of razor blades.

_____

_____

Discussion Questions

Discuss the answers to these questions with your classmates.

1. Who are some of the greatest inventors in history?
2. Name three great inventions of the 20th century. How did they change our lives?
3. If you could invent something, what would it be? How would your invention make life better or easier?

Critical Thinking Questions

Discuss the answers to these questions with your classmates.

1. What are some disposable products that you use? How do they make your life easier? What are some problems caused by disposable products? Do you think we should have more or less disposable products in the future?
2. Gillette knew how to advertise. Today there are advertisements almost everywhere we look. What forms of advertising do we have today? Do you think there are too many advertisements in our daily lives? What are some of the good and bad points about the amount of advertisements in our lives today?

Writing

Writing Skills

A. Using *too* and *very*

Using *too* or *very* + Adjective

Very goes before an adjective. It emphasizes the adjective. It has a positive meaning.

Example:

Gillette had a **very** good idea.

You must not confuse **very** with **too**. When **too** goes before an adjective, it gives the idea of "more than necessary." **Too** has a negative meaning.

Examples:

That razor is **too** sharp. (I don't like it.)

That razor is **very** sharp. (I like it.)

Two Meanings of *too*

Too changes its meaning with the position it has in a sentence. Before an adjective, it has a negative meaning.

Example:

This electric razor is **too** noisy. (I don't like it.)

At the end of an affirmative sentence, **too** means "also."

Example:

An electric razor is heavy, **too**. (It is heavy also.)

Note: You should use a comma before **too** when it means "also."

B. Exercises

1. Complete these sentences with **too** or **very**.

1. This razor is _____ good. I like it.
2. I don't like this razor. It's _____ expensive for me.
3. He likes a strong aftershave. This is _____ weak for him.
4. After he showers and shaves, he looks _____ clean.
5. This aftershave is _____ expensive. I can never buy it.
6. I like electric razors. They are _____ convenient.

2. Rewrite the second sentence in each pair, using **too** in the correct place.

1. I don't like this aftershave. It is stronger than necessary.

Example: It is too strong.

2. That aftershave is expensive. It also has a strong smell.

_____

_____

3. That toothpaste is good for your teeth. It also makes teeth whiter.

_____

_____

4. I didn't buy that toothbrush. It is more expensive than necessary.

_____

_____

5. This shampoo makes my hair soft. It also makes my hair shiny.

_____

_____

6. I don't use that shampoo. It has more chemicals than necessary.

_____

_____

3. Find the mistakes. There are 10 mistakes in grammar and capitalization. Find and correct them.

   The Chinese invent toothbrushes. This toothbrushes had animal hair because there was no nylons at that time. In 1938, people started to use nylon toothbrushes. Today we can buy much types and colors of toothbrushes. But in some african and south american country, people still use Tree branches to care for their tooth.

Writing Practice

A. Write Sentences

Answer these questions with complete sentences.

1. Do you think the toothbrush is a good invention?

_____

_____

2. Do you prefer a regular or an electric toothbrush?

_____

_____

3. Do you use a toothbrush with soft or hard bristles?

_____

_____

4. How often do you buy a new toothbrush or replace the brush of the electric toothbrush?

_____

_____

5. Why do you like or do not like an electric toothbrush? (For example, it cleans your teeth better, or it is heavy and not convenient.)

_____

_____

6. Do you like the idea of a disposable toothbrush? Why or why not?

_____

_____

B. Rewrite in Paragraph Form

Rewrite your sentences in the form of a paragraph. Then use the paragraph checklist to check your work.

Paragraph Checklist

☐ Did you indent the first line?
☐ Did you give your paragraph a title?
☐ Did you write the title with a capital letter or letters?
☐ Did you put the title in the center at the top of the page?
☐ Did you write on every other line?

C. Edit Your Paragraph

Work with a partner or your teacher to edit your sentences. Correct spelling, punctuation, vocabulary, and grammar. Use the editing checklist to help you.

Editing Checklist

- ☐ Subject in every sentence?
- ☐ Verb in every sentence?
- ☐ Words in correct order?
- ☐ Sentences begin with a capital letter?
- ☐ Sentences end with a period directly at the end of a sentence?
- ☐ Sentences have a space between them?
- ☐ Commas in the correct place?
- ☐ Wrong words?
- ☐ Spelling?
- ☐ Missing words (use insertion mark: ^)?

D. Write Your Final Copy

After you edit your paragraph, you can write the final copy.

Weaving It Together

⏱ Timed Writing

Answer these questions with complete sentences. Use capital letters and periods where necessary. You have 50 minutes to answer the questions and rewrite them into paragraph form.

1. Why do you think the cell phone is a good invention?
2. How is it better than the old phone with a cord?
3. For what can you use a cell phone? (phone/texting/photos/e-mail/social networking, etc.)
4. How often do you use your cell phone?
5. Do you think some people use their cell phones in places they should not? Give an example.
6. How does the cell phone help you and make your life better?

Connecting to the Internet

A. Use the Internet to research these products. Find out who invented each product and in what year.
   - microwave oven
   - pop-up toaster
   - gas stove
   - can opener
   - electric blender

B. Jacob Schick invented the first electric razor. Look up Schick on the Internet. Find the answers to the following questions:
   - Where and when was Schick born?
   - What made Schick want to invent an electric razor?
   - How and when did Schick invent the electric razor?
   - What company did Schick form to sell his invention?

What Do You Think Now?

Refer to page 119 at the beginning of this unit. Do you know the answers now? Complete the sentence, or circle the best answer.

1. People saw frozen food in packages for the first time in _____.
2. People liked/didn't like frozen food in packages at first.
3. Birdseye is/is not the name of the person who started a company.
4. Gillette invented a _____ that you could throw away.
5. Gillette had his _____ on every package of razors.

People

What Do You Think?

Answer the questions with your best guess. Circle **Yes** or **No**.

Do you think . . .

1. U.S. President Barack Obama was born in Kenya?   **Yes**   **No**
2. President Obama lived in Hawaii?   **Yes**   **No**
3. President Obama was a lawyer?   **Yes**   **No**
4. the first woman to climb the highest mountain in the world was an American?   **Yes**   **No**
5. the first woman to climb the highest mountain in the world was tall and heavy?   **Yes**   **No**

13 Barack Obama's Road to the Presidency

Pre-Reading

Discuss the answers to these questions with your classmates.

1. What can you tell about this man's personality from the photo?
2. What do you think he is doing?
3. Why is he famous?

Key Vocabulary

Do you know these words? Match the words with the meanings.

1. attended _____
2. candidate _____
3. elected _____
4. graduated _____
5. honest _____
6. humble _____
7. protected _____
8. raise _____

a. guarded; saved from harm
b. look after a child until he or she grows up
c. went to; was present at
d. someone who tries to get chosen for a political position
e. from a lower social class; believing you are not better than other people
f. someone who tells the truth
g. got a degree from a college or university
h. chosen by votes

Reading

Track 13

Barack Obama's Road to the Presidency

1   **B**arack H. Obama is the first African-American president of the United States. He has a **humble** background and believes in hard work, education, and family.

Barack was born in Hawaii in 1961. His mother was a white woman from Kansas. His father was a black man from Kenya. They met at the University of

5   Hawaii and later married. Some years later, his father and mother divorced. His father went back to Kenya and became an economist for the government. His mother married an oil manager from Indonesia. At the age of six, Barack moved to Jakarta with his parents. He lived there until the age of 10. During that time, Barack saw much poverty.

10 Barack and his mother moved back to Hawaii. They lived with his grandparents in a small apartment. Barack's grandparents helped to **raise** him. His grandfather sold furniture, and his grandmother worked in a bank. They taught him the importance of family, education, and hard work.

Barack was a good student. He **attended** Columbia University in New York

15 City with the help of student loans and scholarships. After he **graduated** in 1983, he moved to Chicago. For three years, he helped the city's poor community in the South Side. Then he attended Harvard Law School in Cambridge, Massachusetts. When he graduated in 1991, Barack knew what he wanted to do. He refused a high-paying job. Instead he went back to Chicago and became

20 a lawyer. He helped poor people get their rights to fair housing and jobs.

Eventually Barack became a senator for the state of Illinois. His district included the richest area and the poorest area. He was senator from 1996 to 2004. While he was a state senator, he helped to pass laws. These laws **protected** working families and made the government more **honest**.

25 In 2004, Barack became a U.S. senator. Four years later, in 2008, he became a **candidate** for the president of the United States. By then he was married to Michelle, and they had two daughters, Malia, 10, and Sasha, 7. Barack gave speeches that made people like and admire him. He gave people hope. They wanted change. They **elected** Barack Obama as the

30 44th president on November 4, 2008.

Vocabulary

A. Vocabulary in Context

Complete these sentences with the words below.

attended	candidate	elected
graduated	humble	raise
honest	protect	

1. Barack came from an ordinary, or _____, family.
2. His grandfather and grandmother helped to _____ him in Hawaii.
3. Barack _____ Columbia University in New York. Scholarships and student loans paid for his studies.
4. He _____ from Columbia University in 1983.
5. As a senator, he wanted to _____ poor families.
6. Barack wanted to make the government _____.
7. Barack Obama became a _____ for president.
8. In 2008, Americans _____ Barack Obama as their president.

Word Partnership	Use **protect** with:
n.	protect **against attacks**, protect **children**, protect **citizens**, **duty to** protect, **efforts to** protect, protect **the environment**, **laws** protect, protect **people**, protect **privacy**, protect **property**, protect **women**, protect **workers**
adj.	**designed to** protect, **necessary to** protect, **supposed to** protect

B. Vocabulary in New Context

Answer the questions with complete sentences.

1. Who was elected president of the United States in 2008?

   Example: Barack Obama was elected president of the United States.

2. Who was another candidate for president in 2008?

   _____

   _____

3. Which school are you attending now?

_____

_____

4. From which school did you graduate?

_____

_____

5. Who raised you when you were young?

_____

_____

C. Vocabulary Building

Complete these sentences with the words from the box.

attend (_verb_)	**attendance** (_noun_)

1. We must _____ school every day.

2. Our teacher takes _____ every day to know who is not in class.

graduate (_verb_)	**graduation** (_noun_)

3. My parents came to my _____ ceremony last summer.

4. I want to _____ from college next June.

protect (_verb_)	**protection** (_noun_)

5. It is good to use sunscreen for _____ against the sun.

6. The police _____ the president against attack.

Reading Comprehension

A. Looking for the Main Ideas

Circle the letter of the best answer.

1. Barack loved _____.
   a. law schools and lawyers
   b. to change schools
   c. school and education

2. Before he became president, Barack worked _____.
   a. at high-paying jobs
   b. to get people their rights
   c. as a lawyer for the government

3. People elected Barack Obama because _____.
   a. he gave people hope
   b. he was an African American
   c. he was humble when he spoke

B. Looking for Details

One word in each sentence is not correct. Rewrite the sentence with the correct word.

1. Barack's mother was a white woman from Kenya.

_____

_____

2. Barack's mother married an oil manager from Hawaii.

_____

_____

3. His grandfather sold oil in Hawaii.

_____

_____

4. After he graduated in 1991, Barack went to Chicago and became a senator.

_____

_____

5. In 2004, he became a candidate for the president of the United States.

_____

_____

6. Barack gave speeches that made people like and change him.

_____

_____

Discussion Questions

Discuss the answers to these questions with your classmates.

1. Who is the most famous head of government in your country's history?
2. Why is he or she famous? What good or bad did this leader do for your country?
3. Who is your favorite American president? Why?
4. Do you think the United States will ever have a woman president? Why or why not?

Critical Thinking Questions

Discuss the answers to these questions with your classmates.

1. Would you like to be the leader of a country? Why or why not? If you could be the leader of any country, which country would it be, and why?
2. What do you think are the qualities of a good leader? What should the leader of a country try to do? Do you think a person from any background, ethnic group, or gender should be allowed to become president? Why?

Writing

Writing Skills

A. Writing about Time

Asking Questions

Asking the right questions is important when you write about another person's life. In Exercise 1 on the next page, you will write questions to go with the sentences.

Prepositions of Time

Using *in*

Use **in** with years or months.

Examples:

In 1997, . . .

In December, . . .

Using *from . . . to . . .*

Use **from** for the beginning of an action and **to** for the end of the action.

Examples:

I went to high school **from** 1996 **to** 2001.

I work **from** nine **to** five.

She was on vacation **from** July 15 **to** August 15.

Using *for*

Use **for** to show how long.

Examples:

I studied English **for** three years.

I stayed in New York **for** 10 days.

B. Exercises

1. Write the questions for these answers.

1. _____?

I was born in Tokyo, Japan.

2. _____?

I was born in 1984.

3. _____?

My father is an engineer.

4. _____?

My mother is a homemaker.

5. _____?

I have two brothers and one sister.

6. _____?

I went to high school in Tokyo.

7. _____?

I graduated from high school in 2001.

8. _____?

Right now, I am studying English.

9. _____?

In the future, I want to go to an American university.

10. _____?

I want to study design.

2. Write the correct prepositions in the blanks.

1. I arrived in Boston _____ June for the summer.
2. He lived in Tokyo _____ 16 years.
3. She worked for that company _____ 1995 _____ 2002.
4. He graduated from high school _____ 1998.
5. He worked for that company _____ 15 years.
6. He worked from six in the morning _____ eight at night.
7. Barack Obama was born _____ 1961.
8. I am going back _____ December for my vacation.

3. Find the mistakes. There are 10 mistakes in grammar and capitalization. Find and correct the mistakes.

Barack Obama was born to hawaii, but he attends Columbia University in new york. On 2004, Barack became a senator. In november 4, 2008, he become president of the United States.

Writing Practice

A. Write Sentences

Work with a partner. Find out about your partner's life. Ask questions about the past, the present, and the future. These prompts may help you:

Where/when/you born?
How many/brothers/sisters/have?
When/go/high school?
Where/go/high school?
What/study/now?
Where/study/now?
What/do/in the future?
Why?

Include any other questions you like. Use the answers to write sentences about your partner.

B. Rewrite in Paragraph Form

Rewrite your sentences in the form of a paragraph. Use your partner's name as the title. Then use the paragraph checklist to check your work.

Paragraph Checklist

☐ Did you indent the first line?
☐ Did you give your paragraph a title?
☐ Did you write the title with a capital letter or letters?
☐ Did you put the title in the center at the top of the page?
☐ Did you write on every other line?

C. Edit Your Paragraph

Work with a partner or your teacher to edit your sentences. Correct spelling, punctuation, vocabulary, and grammar. Use the editing checklist to help you.

Editing Checklist

☐ Subject in every sentence?
☐ Verb in every sentence?
☐ Words in correct order?
☐ Sentences begin with a capital letter?
☐ Sentences end with a period directly at the end of a sentence?
☐ Sentences have a space between them?
☐ Commas in the correct place?
☐ Wrong words?
☐ Spelling?
☐ Missing words (use insertion mark: ^)?

D. Write Your Final Copy

After you edit your paragraph, you can write the final copy.

14 Junko Tabei: Climb to the Top

Pre-Reading

Discuss the answers to these questions with your classmates.

1. Describe the woman in the photo.
2. What do you think she is doing?

Key Vocabulary

Do you know these words? Match the word or phrase with the meanings.

1. compete _____
2. crawl _____
3. make a fuss _____
4. ice _____
5. injuries _____
6. raise money _____
7. rescued _____
8. team _____
9. weak _____

a. get excited over something that is not important
b. collect money
c. try to win something or be more successful than someone else
d. physical harm from an accident
e. not strong
f. saved
g. move on hands and knees
h. water that freezes and becomes solid
i. a group of people who work or play together for a purpose

Reading

🔊 Junko Tabei: Climb to the Top
Track 14

1   In 1975, Junko Tabei became the first woman to reach the top of Mount Everest in the Himalaya Mountains. Everest is the highest mountain in the world at 29,035 feet. Junko Tabei is four foot nine inches tall (148 cm).

Junko was born in 1939 and grew up in a small town in the north of
5   Japan. During her childhood, she was thin and **weak**. At age 10, Junko went on a school trip. The students climbed two mountains, and Junko loved it. It wasn't like other sports. She didn't have to **compete** against others. She could climb in her own time and ability.

After Junko graduated from Showa Women's University in Tokyo in 1962,
10   she joined several climbing clubs. But they had mostly male members. Some refused to climb with a woman. In 1965, Junko married a well-known Japanese climber, Masanobu Tabei. Over the years, they climbed all the highest mountains of Japan.

Meanwhile Junko started a woman's climbing club. By 1972, people said
15   she was one of the best mountain climbers in Japan. That year, she was chosen to lead a **team** of women to climb Mount Everest. It took three years for the 15 women to train and **raise money** for their climb. Just after they began to train, Junko gave birth to her daughter.

Finally in 1975, the team traveled to Kathmandu in the Himalayas. They
20   found nine guides to help them climb up the mountain. Everything went well until the morning of May 4. Suddenly a huge amount of snow and **ice** on the side of the mountain fell on them. One guide **rescued** Junko. She rushed to help the others. Everyone was alive but they had **injuries,** including Junko. However, the team decided to continue their climb. Sometimes they had to
25   **crawl** on their hands and knees because of their injuries. About two weeks later, on May 16, Junko reached the summit of the world's highest mountain. Later she said, "I can't understand why men **make all this fuss** about Everest—it's only a mountain."

In 1992, Junko Tabei became the first woman to reach the summits of the
30 highest mountains on all seven continents. She still climbs today, a tiny giant
among the world's climbers.

Vocabulary

A. Vocabulary in Context

Complete these sentences with the words below.

compete	ice	rescued
crawl	injuries	team
make all this fuss	raise money	weak

1. When she was a child, Junko was not strong. She was _____.

2. When you climb a mountain, you don't race, or _____, against
others.

3. Junko was the leader of a group of women, or _____, that
climbed Mount Everest.

4. Junko and her team didn't have enough money, so they had to
_____ for their climb.

5. Snow and _____ fell on Junko, the climbers, and the guides.

6. Junko was lucky. A guide saved, or _____, her.

7. The climbers were alive, but they had _____.

8. They had to walk on their hands and knees, or _____.

9. Junko did not understand why men _____ about Everest.

B. Vocabulary in New Context

Answer the questions with complete sentences.

1. When do people feel weak?

_____

2. What is a sport or game people compete in?

_____

3. What sports team (soccer, baseball, etc.) do you like or support?

_____

4. What drinks do you put ice in?

_____

5. When people have an injury after an accident, what do they do?

_____

6. Why do babies crawl?

_____

C. Vocabulary Building

Complete these sentences with the words from the box.

weak (_adjective_)	**weakness** (_noun_)

1. This coffee has too much water in it. It's _____.
2. I have a _____ for chocolate.

icy (_adjective_)	**ice** (_noun_)

3. We put some _____ in the box to keep the water bottles cool.
4. Be careful! The streets are _____.

fussy (_adjective_)	**fuss** (_noun_)

5. I don't know what to prepare for dinner. Amy is very _____ about her food.
6. He made a big _____ for just one dollar!

Reading Comprehension

A. Looking for the Main Ideas

Circle the letter of the best answer.

1. When Junko was a child, she _____.
   a. wanted to compete against others
   b. was healthy and strong
   c. learned that she loved to climb

2. In 1972, Junko _____.
   a. was chosen to lead a team to climb Mt. Everest
   b. raised enough money for a climb on Mt. Everest
   c. started a women's climbing club

3. During the climb up Mt. Everest, Junko and her team _____.
   a. climbed after they had injuries
   b. had to go back because of their injuries
   c. had an easy time the whole way to the summit

B. Looking for Details

Circle **T** if the sentence is true. Circle **F** if the sentence is false.

1. Junko grew up in a large city in the north of Japan.	T	F
2. Junko and her husband climbed the highest mountains around the world.	T	F
3. The men in the climbing clubs liked to climb with Junko.	T	F
4. The women trained for three years before they climbed Everest.	T	F
5. A big storm caused injuries to the climbers.	T	F
6. After she climbed Everest, Junko continued to climb the highest mountains in the world.	T	F

Discussion Questions

Discuss the answers to these questions with your classmates.

1. What are your favorite sports? If you could play a professional sport, which means you would earn money, what sport would you play? Why?
2. Who are some famous women in sports in the past and today? Are there some sports in which women can compete against men?
3. What special strengths and abilities must a mountain climber have? Would you like to climb a mountain? Why or why not?

Critical Thinking Questions

Discuss the answers to these questions with your classmates.

1. Mountain climbing is dangerous. What are some other dangerous sports? Why do you think people do these dangerous sports? Do you think women should do dangerous sports? Why or why not?
2. Junko did not like to compete with others. Why do you think she felt that way? Are you the type of person who likes to compete? How are people different in this way?

Writing

Writing Skills

A. Telling about Someone's Life

Writing in Present or Past Tense

Read the following facts about Junko Tabei.

The Story of Junko Tabei

1939	Junko is born in a small town in the north of Japan. She is a thin and weak child.
1962	Junko graduates from Showa Women's University in Tokyo.
1965	She marries a well-known Japanese climber, Masanobu Tabei.
1972	People say she is the best mountain climber in Japan. She is chosen to lead a team of women to climb Mount Everest. She gives birth to a daughter.
1975	Junko reaches the summit of Mount Everest.
1992	She becomes the first woman to reach the summits of the highest mountains on the seven continents.

Exercises

1. Write the story of Junko Tabei in the past tense.

1939 _____

_____

1962 _____

_____

1965 _____

_____

1972 _____

_____

1975 _____

_____

1992 _____

_____

2. Now write the story of your life. Use the present tense or the past tense. The following models will help you:

I go (went) to high school/elementary school/college.
I graduate (graduated) from high school/college.

The Story of _____

19 _____ _____

_____

_____

19 _____ _____

_____

_____

19 _____ _____

_____

_____

20 _____ _____

_____

_____

20 _____   _____

              _____

              _____

20 _____   _____

              _____

              _____

20 _____   _____

              _____

              _____

B. Different Ways of Saying *when*

Read the following paragraph about Junko Tabei.

In 1939, Junko is born in a small town in the north of Japan. She is a thin and weak child. In 1962, she graduates from Showa Women's University in Tokyo. In 1965, she marries a well-known Japanese climber, Masanobu Tabei. In 1972, people say she is the best mountain climber in Japan. She is chosen to lead a team of women to climb Mount Everest. In the same year, she gives birth to a daughter. In 1975, she reaches the summit of Mount Everest. In 1992, she becomes the first woman to reach the summits of the highest mountains on seven continents.

In the paragraph above, there are too many sentences that begin in the same way:

In 1962, . . .
In 1965, . . .
In 1972, . . .
In 1975, . . .

Underline the sentences in the paragraph above that begin this way. We can change some of them in the following ways:

In 1962, . . .	At age 23, When she is 23,
In 1965, . . .	At age 26, When she is 26, Three years later,
In 1972, . . .	At age 33, When she is 33, Seven years later,
In 1975, . . .	Three years later, At age 36, When she is 36,
In 1992, . . .	Seventeen years later, At age 53, When she is 53,

Exercises

3. Look at the same paragraph about Junko Tabei. Use a different beginning in each of the blank spaces.

In 1939, Junko is born in a small town in the north of Japan. She is a thin and weak child. **1.** _____, she graduates from Showa Women's University in Tokyo. **2.** _____, she marries a well-known Japanese climber, Masanobu Tabei. **3.** _____, people say she is the best mountain climber in Japan. She is chosen to lead a team of women to climb Mount Everest. In the same year, she gives birth to a daughter. **4.** _____, she reaches the summit of Mount Everest. **5.** _____, she becomes the first woman to reach the summits of the highest mountains on seven continents.

4. Find the mistakes. There are 10 mistakes in grammar and capitalization. Find and correct them.

Mount Everest is the highest mountain in the world. She is in the Himalaya Mountains between tibet and nepal, north of india. Many people try to get to the summit of Mount Everest, but they couldn't. In 1953, edmund hillary and tenzig norgay are the first to reach the summit.

Writing Practice

A. Rewrite in Paragraph Form

Step 1: Rewrite the sentences about your life (see pages 163–164) in the form of a paragraph.

Step 2: Rewrite your paragraph again with only one "In 19_____" at the beginning of a sentence. Use other words with the same meaning. Then use the paragraph checklist to check your work.

Paragraph Checklist

☐ Did you indent the first line?
☑ Did you give your paragraph a title?
☐ Did you write the title with a capital letter or letters?
☐ Did you put the title in the center at the top of the page?
☐ Did you write on every other line?

B. Edit Your Paragraph

Work with a partner or your teacher to edit your sentences. Correct spelling, punctuation, vocabulary, and grammar. Use the editing checklist to help you.

Editing Checklist

- ☐ Subject in every sentence?
- ☐ Verb in every sentence?
- ☐ Words in correct order?
- ☐ Sentences begin with a capital letter?
- ☐ Sentences end with a period directly at the end of a sentence?
- ☐ Sentences have a space between them?
- ☐ Commas in the correct place?
- ☐ Wrong words?
- ☐ Spelling?
- ☐ Missing words (use insertion mark: ^)?

C. Write Your Final Copy

After you edit your paragraph, you can write the final copy.

Weaving It Together

⏱ Timed Writing

Write the story of a family member. Use the format from Exercise 2 on page 163 to help you. Rewrite your sentences in paragraph form. Use only one "In 19_____" at the beginning of a sentence. Use other words with the same meaning. You have 50 minutes.

Connecting to the Internet

A. Use the Internet to look up **2** of the following world leaders of the past. Find out when and where the person was born, who the person's parents were, and what made that person famous.

- Alexander the Great
- Mustafa Kemal Atatürk
- Simon Bolivar
- Napoleon Bonaparte
- Winston Churchill
- Vladimir Lenin
- Mohandas Gandhi
- Nelson Mandela
- Franklin Roosevelt
- Mao Zedong

B. Use the Internet to find out about some "great firsts." For what are the following five women famous for doing first? In what year did they achieve it?

- Anne Bradstreet
- Mary Kies
- Lucy Walker
- Kathryn Sullivan
- Mae Carol Jemison

What Do You Think Now?

Refer to page 145 at the beginning of this unit. Do you know the answers now? Complete the sentence, or circle the best answer.

1. President Obama was born in _____.
2. President Obama lived/didn't live in Hawaii.
3. President Obama was/was not a lawyer.
4. The first woman to climb the highest mountain in the world was _____.
5. The first woman to climb the highest mountain in the world was/was not big.

Readings from Literature

What Do You Think?

Answer the questions with your best guess. Circle **Yes** or **No**.

Do you think . . .

1. poems always follow rules of sound or rhyme?		**Yes**	**No**
2. English-language students like you can write a poem?		**Yes**	**No**
3. every country has fables?		**Yes**	**No**
4. Aesop is famous for his fables?		**Yes**	**No**
5. fables are stories about animals?		**Yes**	**No**

Chapter 15 The Poetry of Rain

Pre-Reading

Discuss the answers to these questions with your classmates.

1. Describe what you see in the picture.
2. How do you feel when it rains?
3. What kind of weather do you like the most?
4. What kind of weather do you not like?

Key Vocabulary

Do you know these words? Match the words or phrases with the meanings.

1. to beat _____
2. to bounce _____
3. to spill _____
4. gutters _____
5. to lick _____
6. tin _____
7. to bang _____

a. to rub the tongue over, as you do when you eat ice cream
b. to hit in a way that makes a sharp, loud noise
c. to hit again and again
d. a kind of metal
e. open pipes on a roof that catch and carry rain water
f. to hit so that the object (like a ball) comes back
g. to flow over

Reading

"Rain" by Dionne Brand

Track 15

1   It finally came,
    it **beat** on the house
    it **bounced** on the flowers
    it **banged** on the **tin** roof
5   it rolled in the **gutters**
    it made the street muddy
    it **spilled** on the village
    it **licked** all the windows
    it jumped on the hill.
10 It stayed for two days
    and then it left.

Vocabulary

A. Vocabulary in Context

Complete these sentences with the words below.

banged	spilled	bounced	licked
beat	gutters	tin	

1. The rain made a loud noise when it hit the roof. It _____ on the roof.
2. The roof was made of _____.
3. The _____ around the roof took the water from the roof to the street below.
4. The rain _____ on the village, like water flowing out of a glass that was too full.
5. The rain hit the house over and over again. It _____ on the house.

6. Like a ball hitting a wall, the rain _____ on the flowers.

7. The rain, like a cat's tongue, _____ the windows.

Word Partnership	Use **beat** with:
n.	beat **a rug, heart** beat, beat **eggs**
prep.	beat **against**, beat **on, on/to a** beat

B. Vocabulary in New Context

Choose the correct answer. Then use the answer in a complete sentence.

1. What object usually bounces?

an apple   a ball   a flower

Example: <u>A ball usually bounces</u>.

2. What things do we usually lick?

stamps   windows   flowers

3. Where do you see gutters?

on a car   on a house   on a train

4. What do we beat?

a drum   a chair   a book

5. What can bang?

a cloud   a door   snow

C. Vocabulary Building

Complete these sentences with the best answer. Look up the new words in your dictionary.

1. It is difficult to drive because there are _____ of fog.

a. sheets   b. patches   c. clouds

2. I don't listen to the weather _____ because it is usually wrong.

a. warning   b. news   c. forecast

3. Sunscreen gives you protection against the harmful effects of the sun's _____.

a. rays   b. waves   c. strokes

4. There are scattered _____ all day today, so we can go out. We just have to take an umbrella in case.

a. breezes   b. showers   c. rains

Reading Comprehension

Answer these questions with complete sentences.

1. What does *it* mean in the poem?

_____

_____

2. What kind of place do you think the poem describes?

_____

_____

3. How long did it rain?

_____

_____

4. Was it a light rain or a strong rain?

_____

_____

5. Were people waiting for the rain to come?

_____

_____

6. The rain in the poem is like an animal or a person. What animal do you think it can be? Why?

_____

_____

Discussion Questions

Discuss the answers to these questions with your classmates.

1. Which words in the poem did you like most? Why? Which words did you dislike?
2. Draw a picture of the scene in the poem and show it to your classmates.
3. Read the poem aloud. Decide which words to say more loudly. What effect do you think this has?

Critical Thinking Questions

Discuss the answers to these questions with your classmates.

1. Do you like poetry? Why or why not? How are songs like poems? How are poems like paintings?
2. If you had to write a poem about a snowstorm, what words would you use? What pictures would you try to create in the mind of the reader? Do the same for a sandstorm.

Writing

Writing Skills

A. Review of Parts of Speech

A *noun* is a word that names a person, place, or thing.

Examples:

man   Mexico   school

A *verb* is a word that describes an action or a state. Every sentence has a verb. Verbs change forms depending on tense and number.

Examples:

teach, taught   look, looked   I see, he sees

An *adjective* describes a noun or a pronoun.

Examples:

a **hot** day   **wet** streets   a **dark** sky

An *adverb* describes a verb, an adjective, or another adverb.

Examples:

The sun shines **brightly**.
The snow fell **gently**.

B. Exercises

1. Circle the correct answer.

1. Which is a noun?
warm   snowed   sky

2. Which is a noun?
covered   flowers   bright

3. Which is a noun?
gentle   wet   snowstorm

4. Which is a verb?

burned   hot   noisily

5. Which is a verb?

dark   softly   blew

6. Which is a verb?

fast   whistled   rainy

7. Which is an adjective?

cold   storm   shone

8. Which is an adjective?

blizzard   sunny   froze

9. Which is an adjective?

poured   strongly   skinny

10. Which is an adverb?

cloudy   noisily   dry

11. Which is an adverb?

violently   whispered   roared

12. Which is an adverb?

freezing   muddy   brilliantly

2. Look at the four weather words below. Then write three verbs, two adjectives, one adverb, and one prepositional phrase that go with each one.

Noun	snow	wind	rain	sun
Verb	to snow			
Verb				
Verb				
Adjective				
Adjective				
Adverb				
Prepositional Phrase				

Writing Practice

How to Write a Poem about Weather

Use the words in Exercise 2 to create your own weather poem. Read the instructions and look at the example.

Instructions	Example
Write a weather noun on the first line.	Snow
Write two adjectives on the second line.	Soft, white
Write two –ing verbs on the third line.	Falling, covering
Write an adverb and a prepositional phrase on the fourth line.	Gently through the night
Write the noun from the first line again.	Snow

Chapter 16 More than Just a Story

Pre-Reading

Discuss the answers to these questions with your classmates.

1. Fables are stories that give a message about life. Every country has fables. Do you know any?
2. Proverbs are one or two sentences that give a message about life. For example, *The grass is always greener on the other side of the fence*. Which do you prefer—proverbs or fables?

Key Vocabulary

Do you know these words? Match the words or phrases with the meanings.

1. to quarrel _____
2. to determine _____
3. to fetch _____
4. a bundle of _____
5. to convince _____
6. united _____
7. to undo _____

a. to open up or untie
b. to persuade someone
c. to argue or fight with words
d. together
e. to decide
f. to go and get
g. a bunch or group of

Reading

Track 16

"Father and Sons"

This reading is one of Aesop's fables. Aesop was an African slave. He went to Greece around the year 600 B.C. (before Christ) and wrote 350 stories for adults that teach lessons about life.

1   **A** certain man had several sons who were always **quarreling** with each other. However hard he tried, he could not get them to live together in peace. So he **determined** to **convince** them of their stupidity in the following way. He told them to **fetch a bundle of** sticks and asked each son in turn to break
5   it across his knee. All tried and failed. Then he **undid** the bundle, and gave them the sticks one by one. They had no difficulty breaking them. "There, my boys," he said. "**United** you will have power. But if you quarrel and separate, you will be weak."

Vocabulary

A. Vocabulary in Context

Complete these sentences with the words below.

a bundle of	determined	undid
convinced	quarreled	united
fetch		

1. The sons never agreed with one another. They _____.
2. The father _____ to make his sons work together and be happy together.
3. The father _____ his sons that what they were doing was not good.
4. He told them to _____ some sticks.
5. The sons could not break _____ sticks.
6. The father _____ the bundle of sticks and gave each son one.
7. The father told his sons that _____ they will be strong.

B. Vocabulary Building

Match the words in Column A with those in Column B. There may be more than one possibility. Then make sentences with each correct combination.

A	B
1. a bundle of	a. matches
2. a box of	b. tools
3. a pack of	c. flowers
4. a bunch of	d. sticks
5. a set of	e. pants
6. a pair of	f. cards

C. Vocabulary in New Context

Answer the questions with complete sentences.

1. Who often tells you to fetch something?

Example: _My grandmother often tells me to fetch her glasses._

_____

_____

2. With what people did you quarrel recently?

_____

_____

3. What are you determined to do in the future?

_____

_____

4. Who convinces you to work hard at school?

_____

_____

5. What do you have a bundle of?

_____

_____

6. On what piece of clothing do you undo buttons?

_____

_____

Reading Comprehension

Answer these questions with complete sentences.

1. How many sons did the man have?

_____

_____

2. What problem did the sons have?

_____

_____

3. What did the father tell them to do?

_____

_____

4. What did the sons try to do?

_____

_____

5. What happened?

_____

_____

6. What was the father's advice?

_____

_____

7. What is the meaning of the story? Circle the correct answer.
   a. You are stronger when you work alone.
   b. You are stronger together.
   c. Argument is bad.

Discussion Questions

Discuss the answers to these questions with your classmates.

1. Can a parent give good advice?
2. Why is it sometimes difficult to work in a team?
3. What kind of person works well in a team?

Critical Thinking Questions

Discuss the answers to these questions with your classmates.

1. What are some common lessons that fables teach us? Do you think fables are a good way to teach people about life? What are some other ways in which we are taught moral lessons?
2. In the past, elders told stories to children in order to teach them about life and morals. Today young people learn from television, movies, video games, and the Internet. In what ways is this good? In what ways is it bad?

Writing

Writing Skills

A. Paraphrasing

When you paraphrase a sentence, you say the same thing in your own words. It is useful to look in a dictionary of synonyms or a thesaurus to find a different word with the same meaning.

Examples:

Sentence: <u>However hard he tried</u>, he could not <u>get</u> his sons to live <u>together in peace</u>.

Paraphrase: He tried very hard, but he could not make his sons live with each other without fighting.

B. Exercises

1. Paraphrase these lines from the reading by replacing the underlined words. (Look back at the key vocabulary if you need help.)

1. So he <u>determined</u> to <u>convince</u> them of their stupidity.

_____

_____

2. He told them to <u>fetch a bundle of</u> sticks.

_____

_____

3. <u>United</u> you will <u>have power</u>.

_____

_____

4. If you <u>quarrel</u> and separate, you will <u>be weak</u>.

_____

_____

2. Every proverb has a meaning. Rewrite the proverb in your own words. When you are finished, show your sentences to your partner and compare your answers.

1. Proverb: In many words, a lie or two may escape.

   Rewrite: _When I talk too much, I may tell a lie._

2. Proverb: You scratch my back and I'll scratch yours.

   Rewrite: _____

   _____

3. Proverb: Look before you leap.

   Rewrite: _____

   _____

4. Proverb: Actions speak louder than words.

   Rewrite: _____

   _____

5. Proverb: Children are a poor man's wealth.

   Rewrite: _____

   _____

3. Find the mistakes. There are 10 mistakes in grammar and capitalization. Find and correct them.

We do not know two much about Aesop because he lived a long time ago. He lived in africa. He was not a freely man; he was a Slave. Later, he became a freely man and went to greece. There, he worked for the king as an ambassador. When he worked for the king, some people get angry at him, and killed him. But Aesop did not do anything wrong. Later, they made a Statue of Aesop in greece to remember Him.

Writing Practice

Work alone, in pairs, or in groups. Write three proverbs from your country. Then rewrite each proverb in your own words.

Weaving It Together

⏱ Timed Writing

Write the fable of "Father and Sons" in your own words in paragraph form. Don't forget to use capital letters and periods where necessary. You have 50 minutes.

Connecting to the Internet

A. Use the Internet to find the poem "April Rain Song" by Langston Hughes. What is the poem about? What pictures does it create in your mind? Now use the Internet to find a poem by your favorite poet. Read the poem aloud to your classmates and explain why you like it.

B. Use the Internet to find two other fables that Aesop wrote. Which animals appear in these stories? Which animals appear most often in these stories? Choose two fables and tell what lessons they teach.

What Do You Think Now?

Refer to page 169 at the beginning of this unit. Do you know the answers now? Complete the sentence, or circle the best answer.

1. Poems always follow/don't always follow rules of sound or rhyme.
2. English-language students like you can/cannot write a poem.
3. Every country has _____.
4. Aesop is famous for his _____.
5. Fables are/are not stories about animals.

Photo Credits

This page constitutes an extension of the copyright page. We have made every effort to trace the ownership of all copyrighted material and to secure permission from copyright holders. In the event of any question arising as to the use of any material, we will be pleased to make the necessary corrections in future printings. Thanks are due to the following authors, publishers, and agents for permission to use the material indicated.

Chapter 1. 1: center, © Danny Lehman/Corbis; right, © Bob Krist/CORBIS; top left, © Sean Prior/Shutterstock **2:** © Dmitriy Shironosov/Shutterstock

Chapter 2. 12: © Vakhrushev Pavel/Shutterstock

Chapter 3. 25: bottom right, © Neale Cousland/Shutterstock; left, © CSLD/Shutterstock; top right, © Galyna Andrushko/Shutterstock **26:** © Joseph Calev/Shutterstock

Chapter 4. 37: © Gavin Hellier/JAI/Corbis

Chapter 5. 51: © Vibrant Image Studio/Shutterstock **52:** © John Wollwerth/Shutterstock

Chapter 6. 61: © Studio 37/Shutterstock

Chapter 7. 73: © Atlantide Phototravel/Corbis **74:** © Gideon Mendel/CORBIS

Chapter 8. 85: © Alain Evrard/Impact Photos/Imagestate

Chapter 9. 97: © Hannamariah/Shutterstock **98:** © Carolina K. Smith, M.D. RF/Shutterstock

Chapter 10. 109: © Beau Lark/Corbis

Chapter 11. 119: © Stephanie Maze/CORBIS **120:** © altrendo images/Getty Images

Chapter 12. 131: right, right, © Monkey Business Images/Shutterstock **131:** right, © AP Images/Gillette Photos

Chapter 13. 145: bottom left, © AP Images/David Parker **145:** top right, right, © AP Images/Chris Polk **145:** top left, © AP Images/John Smierciak **146:** © AP Images/Ron Edmonds

Chapter 14. 156: © AP Images/Binod Joshi

Chapter 15. 169: © sergey makarenko/Shutterstock **170:** © Craig Tuttle/CORBIS

Chapter 16. 178: The Bundle of Sticks, illustration from 'Baby's Own Aesop', engraved and printed by Edmund Evans, London, published c.1920 (colour litho), Crane, Walter (1845–1915) (after)/Private Collection/Ken Welsh/The Bridgeman Art Library

Skills Index

Grammar and Usage

Listening/Speaking

Reading

Technology—Internet

Test-taking Skills

Circle best answer, 4, 6, 14, 24, 28, 29, 39, 54, 55, 63, 65, 100, 102, 111–112, 124, 150, 160, 168, 172–173, 175–176, 182, 186

Critical thinking questions, 7, 17, 31, 42, 56, 66, 79, 90, 103, 113, 125, 137, 151, 161, 174, 182

Discussion questions, 2, 7, 12, 17, 26, 31, 37, 41–42, 52, 56, 66, 74, 79, 85, 90, 98, 103, 109, 113, 120, 125, 131, 137, 146, 151, 156, 161, 170, 174, 178, 182

Fill in the blank, 104, 122, 148, 149, 154, 158, 159, 171–172, 179

Matching, 2, 12, 26, 37, 52, 61, 74, 81, 85, 98, 109, 120, 131, 146, 156, 170, 178, 180

Multiple-choice questions, 6, 29–30, 55, 65, 100, 102, 112, 124

Sentence completion, 4–5, 11, 14–16, 20–21, 24, 28–29, 33–35, 39–41, 44–48, 50, 54–55, 59, 63, 65–66, 76–78, 81–83, 87–88, 89, 92, 95, 105, 112, 118, 122–123, 128–129, 133–136, 139–141, 144, 148–151, 158–159, 168, 171–173, 179, 180–182, 186

Sentence rewrite, 16, 30–31, 67–68, 139–140

True-or-false questions, 6, 41, 56, 78, 89, 102, 113, 124, 160

Yes or no questions, 1, 25, 51, 73, 97, 119, 145, 169

Topics

Customs, 73–95
    Naming babies, 73–84
    Thailand customs, 85–95
Food, 97–118
    Chocolate, 97–108
    Coffee, 109–118
Health, 51–72
    Laughter, 61–72
    Sleep, 51–60
Inventions, 119–144
    Frozen food, 119–130
    Razors, 131–144
People, 145–168
    Barack Obama, 145–155
    Junko Tabei, 156–168
Places, 26–50
    Dubai, 26–46
    Iceland, 37–50
Readings from literature, 169–186
    Fables, 178–186
    Poetry of rain, 169–177

Special days, 1–24
    Birthdays, 2–11
    New Year's, 12–24

Vocabulary

Building, 5, 14–15, 29, 40, 55, 64, 77–78, 88, 101–102, 112, 134–135, 149, 159, 180

In context, 4–5, 14, 15, 28–29, 39–40, 54, 63–64, 76–77, 87–88, 100–101, 111, 122–123, 133–134, 148–149, 158–159, 171–172, 179–181

Key, 2, 12, 26, 37, 52, 61, 74, 85, 98, 109, 120, 131, 146, 156, 170, 178

Writing

About someone's life, 162–164
Asking questions, 152
Capitalization, 9, 19, 34
Comparison
    as...as for, 126
    Comparative form of adjectives, 43, 44–45
    Superlative form of adjectives, 43–47
Exercises, 9–10, 19, 33–34, 44–47, 57, 67–68, 81–82, 92, 104–105, 114–115, 126–128, 138–139, 153–154, 162–163, 165, 175–176, 183–184
Finding and correcting mistakes, 10, 19, 34, 47, 58, 69, 82, 92, 106, 140, 166, 185
Instruction writing, 104
Paragraphs, 21–23, 35, 49, 60, 70–71, 84, 94, 107–108, 116–117, 129–130, 141–142, 155, 166–167
Paraphrasing, 183–184
Poetry, 177
Practice, 185
Prepositional phrase, 91–92
Prepositions of time, 152–153
Present or past tense writing, 162–164
Proverbs, 184
Sentences, 11, 20, 34–35, 47–48, 59, 69–70, 83, 93, 106–107, 115–116, 128–129, 140–141, 154–155
    Order of, 18–19
    Punctuation, 9
    Subject, 8
    Verbs, 8, 175–176
Syllables, 44
Timed writing, 24, 50, 72, 95, 118, 143, 168, 186
Writing about time, 152–153